T0290164

The New
Social Game

Davide Pellegrini
Francesca De Canio

B
U
P

Sharing Economy and Digital
Revolution: Into the Change
of Consumers' Habits

Typesetting: Laura Panigara, Cesano Boscone (MI)

Copyright © 2017 Bocconi University Press
EGEA S.p.A.

EGEA S.p.A.
Via Salasco, 5 - 20136 Milano
Tel. 02/5836.5751 – Fax 02/5836.5753
egea.edizioni@unibocconi.it – www.egeaeditore.it

First Edition: June 2017

ISBN International Edition 978-88-85486-15-7
ISBN Moby pocket Edition 978-88-85486-17-1
ISBN Epub Edition   978-88-85486-16-4
ISBN Domestic Edition   978-88-99902-03-2

Print: Digital Print Service, Segrate (MI)

Table of Contents

Preface

Since the onset of the digital revolution, the traditional divide between value creation – *research and development, production and advertising* – and value distribution – *sales, use and post-use* – has been blurring. If we consider the impact of digitalization in value chains we find a new and active role for the customer in the value processes. Individuals and companies are increasingly invited to exchange multiple inputs and outputs before, during and after sales. The new contemporaneity and continuity in the creation, distribution and consumption of products and services is gradually leading to a new social game between parties. Companies are able to promote, intermediate and intercept customer conversations, while individuals are able to keep companies under non-contractual observation. Consequently, the new overlap of *social interaction* and *sale* can generate a positive loop between corporate and individual responsibility which brings the market and society closer together.

Nevertheless, the increasing attempts by companies to promote, intermediate and intercept individual conversations is opening up a new ideological debate: is the new social game bringing new value for the gamers? Are individuals acting as customers or as citizens? Is their work being properly compensated? And lastly, are we seeing a truly new form of value co-creation or simply a new form of exploitation?

This work examines theoretical implications of the growing overlap between dialogue and sales, between the market and society or, more simply, between Money and Gift. A review of recent literature is followed by a discussion of logics and empirical evidence, which leads into a focus on the convergence currently taking place between the roles of the customer and the citizen. We develop a new theory of convergence and test it through a specially developed model of a "co-value chain". The model is applied to a large number of recent case studies, providing a topical focus on implications for management.

The findings of our qualitative analysis are confirmed by our quantitative analysis: the active role of consumers in the new co-value chain involves individuals and their expectations about money and gift benefits. This leads to a growing interest on the part of the consumer in being a dynamic actor in the value chain. Companies are thus taking a minor role, as consumers become both producers and users of services. In many cases, companies are mere facilitators of the service, while consumers are channel leaders and drivers of service production and consumption. This phenomenon of *collaborative consumption* is investigated in detail in the empirical section at the end of the book, which conducts an analysis of BlaBlaCar and Airbnb.

Davide Pellegrini
Francesca De Canio

1 The new social game

The active role of the consumer in value creation

Before the digital revolution, the three phases of "proposition – sale – use" followed a clear logical and chronological sequence in time and space: production, distribution and consumption were linear steps in the supply chain.

1. Once upon a time

Nowadays, as time and space constraints are disappearing, companies and customers can exchange inputs before, during and after consumption. Consequently, the traditional divide between value creation – R&D (Research and Development), production and advertising – and value distribution – sales and use – is losing its distinction. The new contemporaneity and continuity of the value processes in the creation, distribution and consumption of both products and services has unexpected implications for economic theories.

Typically, in the past there was a clear theoretical distinction between the roles of value production by companies, and value reception by consumers – the two roles never overlapped. Companies made the proposal – *value proposition* – while consumers purchased – *exchange value* – and used products and services – *value in use.*

Consequently, economic literature assigned the role of value creator to companies, which bear costs of R&D, as well as advertising, before the phases of sale and use – *value distribution* (Bain, 1959; Posner, 1962). In this view, consumers choose goods and services offered by firms and indirectly encourage interbrand competition. This horizontal competition however is accompanied by vertical intrabrand competition, between firms working at various stages of the supply chain. Producers, traders and retailers all try to negotiate the best price to transfer to the consumer downstream (Porter, 1976; Albion, 1983). In fact, the value proposition produces effective value through the vertical network of contacts and relationships established during the phases of *sale-exchange value* (Rosemberg, 1976; Schmalensee, 1989; Hart, 1990; Rispoli, 1998; Snehota and Tunisini, 1999; Valdani, Ancari and Castaldo, 2001). Firms are consequently taking the measure of their informational asymmetries and deciding which processes to internalize or insource -*make*- and which to externalise or outsource -*buy*. The *make or buy dilemma* re-shapes the value chains (Williamson, 1975; Stern El Ansary, 1978).

When the cost of processing information is revolutionized by digital transformation, all the traditional paradigms of industrial economics need to be revisited. What is really changing is that the consumer is now an active protagonist of value creation, rather than affecting it only indirectly. Firms can thus externalize certain value creation processes to the consumer, in a new form of crowdsourcing. In fact, they can invite consumers to cooperate before, during and after sales.

From a theoretical point of view, crowdsourcing is becoming significant in that it is shifting the boundary between the roles of producer and consumer.

Figure 1   Consumer switching in searching and purchasing between online and offline channels

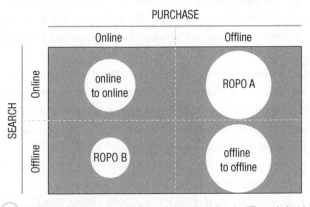

Size indicates share of total sales and show deviations in different industries

In Figure 1 we observe that customers behaviour is influenced by the type of products or services requested. In many cases we see customers who are attracted by a pure digital experience since they research information online and purchase products or services online. In cases conversely we see also *Brick* & *Mortar* behaviour, that is customers who request physical support before, during and after sales – Research offline & Purchase offline –. More often we see a new mix of *Brick* & *Click* expectations which feed new forms of collaboration – Research online & Purchase offline or Research offline & Purchase online –.

2.   The crowdsourcing perspective

The idea that *consumption implies work* has been widely accepted since the time of classical economics. In the 1980s the term "prosumption", which indicates consumers' production for their own consumption, entered Toffler's marketing dictionary. But, while in the past consumers were involved only during the phases of sale and consumption, today they are actively involved right from the planning, production and communication phases. In table 1 we describe how companies can outsource functions to customers in many different processes.

We observe at least seven processes of crowdsourcing (*Co-planning, Co-production, Co-advertising, Co-selling, Co-logistics, Co-use, Co-postuse*), and three combinations of conversations: *one-to-many (O2M), many-to-many (M2M)* and *peer-to-peer (P2P)*.

Table 1   The process of value creation before and after the digital revolution

In the past...		Today...	
Company	Customer	Company	Customer
R&D Planning	–	R&D Planning	Co-planning
Production	–	Production	Co-production
Advertising	–	Advertising	Co-advertising
Selling	Buying	Selling	Co-selling
Logistics	Use	Logistic	Co-use
Post-sales	Post-sale	Post-sale	Co-post-sale

The difference between the three combinations depends on the role of the actors. Let's look at the example of car sharing services.

Table 2   The co-value chain

One-to-many (O2M)		Many-to-many (M2M)		Peer-to-peer (P2P)	
One supplier	Enjoy	**Many** suppliers	Drivers	**Peer** supplier	Citizen
One informediary	**ENJOY**	One infomediary	**UBER**	One infomediary	**BLABLACAR**
Many buyers	Customers	**Many** buyers	Customers	**Peer** buyers	Customers

First we can observe that in the case of a car sharing service like Enjoy, the promoter is also the supplier of the service, so the model is clearly one-to-many (Enjoy to customers).

Conversely in the case of a private taxi service platform like Uber, the promoter is simple aggregating many private professional suppliers in a many-to-many framework (Uber to drivers and customers).

Finally, in a platform like BlaBlaCar the promoter aggregates not professional players but citizens in a peer-to-peer perspective (BlaBlaCar to citizens). In this case the consumer plays the double role of producer and user of the service. This type of sharing business model is called collaborative consumption and will better explained in the following chapters.

Nevertheless, what differences are there from the point of view of individuals? Are individuals aware of the difference between a car sharing service like Enjoy, a private taxi service platform like Uber and a peer-to-peer platform like BlaBlaCar?

3.   Much more than sharing

Before answering, we need to look more closely at the difference between the sharing economy and collaborative consumption.

The sharing economy covers all economic activities where people are directly or indirectly engaged in the creation of economic value. It includes sharing activities in the creation, production, distribution, trade and consumption of goods and services (Matofska, 2014). The models of cooperation that we have called one-to-many and many-to-many clearly refer to the sharing economy. On the other hand, peer-to-peer collaboration appears to be a particular branch of the sharing economy, and we call it *collaborative consumption* (Belk, 2014). The principle difference is explained by the participants' expectations.

In a peer-to-peer platform customers are conscious of being absolute protagonists of the value creation and are committed to the new social game of being customers and citizens at the same. This circumstance influences their satisfaction and loyalty to the platform.

From a theoretical point of view, the new active role played by individuals during collaborative consumption cannot be analysed purely as an economic activity. What we are seeing is in fact a new business model imprinted by a new combination of citizen points of view, that we'll call *society or gift perspective,* and customer points of view, that we'll call *market or money perspective.* The new mix of money and gift expectations drives both the contents and shape of conversation. This is leading to a renewed social sensitivity and is gradually bringing about a new convergence between the market and society. Companies and customers maintain separate and complementary roles, but their conversation is being fundamentally remodelled in both content and shape.

4.   The ideological debate

In light of the new transactional schemes many authors suggest caution. Humphreys and Grayson (2008), for example, suggest that *use value* and *exchange value* should be considered separately, as in fact the situation is different when consumers produce something that they themselves do not use but can be sold to others (exchange value). They argue that when consumers create *use value,* for example when they dispense their own soft drink at a fast-food restaurant or they assemble their own furniture for Ikea, their fundamental role in the economic system does not change. Conversely their role clearly changes when they produce new exchangeable value. These researchers claim that exploitation no longer takes place in factories but is moving into the home, where individuals generate production but are not rewarded by the distribution of the value they have created. Is this true in the case of Enjoy, Uber or BlaBlaCar? The authors often cite the case of the Huffington Post, the digital newspaper with free content supplied by readers and advertising revenues collected by the publisher. In this example thousands of bloggers promoted a class action against the Huffington Post, claiming the publisher refused to make fair payments despite profiting from their advertising revenues. Many authors suggest that consumers have a unique ability to defend themselves against firms, which try to reduce their role to a sort of "part-time employee" of the service provider or a human resource at its disposal (Mills and Morris, 1986; Bowen and Schneider, 1988; Bateson, 1983; Keh and Teo, 2001; Kelley, Skinner and Donnelly, 1992; Zeithaml and Bitner, 2000).

5.   The goal of our research

Imagine that you are a brilliant Ph.D. student in economics. There is a call for participation in a research game promoted by the website Innocentive. com, one of the most important platforms for co-research, and your colleagues advise you to take a look at the website. The following is posted on the home page "… become a *solver*. As a *solver*, you can apply your expertise, stretch your intellectual and creative boundaries, and win cash prizes from $5,000 to $1,000,000 for solving problems in a variety of domains that run the gamut from corporate to humanitarian". Exploring the website, you discover in the comment section that the name Innocentive is a conflation of the words Innovation and Incentive. The website is heavily sponsored by the pharmaceutical industry as well as other commercial enterprises.

Your colleagues say you should submit your ideas to the site, but you have doubts. Will Innocentive exploit your skills and know-how and will they sell your ideas for their own profit? What are the pros and cons of this opportunity?

The research described in this book aims to measure what determinants drive customer choice between one service or another.

In order to answer this question we develop a new theory of convergence and test it through a specially developed model of a "co-value chain". The model is applied to a large number of recent case histories, providing a topical focus on implications for management. In the empirical section at the end of the book we conduct a quantitative analysis of BlaBlaCar and Airbnb.

The final goal of the research is to measure to what extent the gift perspective will influence the money perspective. The answers to these questions will determine the prevailing model of the new social game in the future. We know that the Ford society has disappeared, but will future generations live in an Enjoy or Uber society, or will a BlaBlaCar or Airbnb society prevail?

2   Consumption implies work

Sharing platforms and peer-to-peer communities

When consumers are called to work the co-value architecture are completely reshaped.

This chapter starts clustering 21 cases according to the processes involved – *top down or bottom up schemes* – and the numbers of players – *O2M, M2M or P2P*.

Table 1   Type of player for each type of collaboration

CO-PLANNING	one-to-many	CROWDWORX
	many-to-many	INNOCENTIVE
	peer-to-peer	CITY2.0
CO-PRODUCTION	one-to-many	HUFFINGTON POST
	many-to-many	GIGWALK
	peer-to-peer	AMAZON TURK
CO-ADVERTISING	one-to-many	DUCATI
	many-to-many	ZOOPA
	peer-to-peer	PINTEREST
CO-SELLING	one-to-many	THREADLESS
	many-to-many	GROUPON
	peer-to-peer	FAB
CO-LOGISTICS	one-to-many	ENJOY
	many-to-many	DELIVEROO
	peer-to-peer	WAZE

CO-USE	one-to-many	W. of WARCRAFT
	many-to-many	KHAN ACADEMY
	peer-to-peer	NEXTDOOR
CO-POST-USE	one-to-many	NINTENDO
	many-to-many	TRIPADVISOR
	peer-to-peer	PIRATE BAY

1.   Co-planning

The first group of social games focuses on pre-sale activities and particularly on the collaboration between companies and customers during the co-planning phases.

One-to-many Co-planning: Crowdworx

The first case we examine is CrowdWorx. The homepage shows the main aim of the website: "a social forecasting tool which utilizes the knowledge of your employees and transforms it to quantitative forecasts about sales, new products, and other key business performance indicators".

The business model underpinning CrowdWorx is clearly *one-to-many*, due to the connection of one company and many employees. It acts as a third party that offers a service platform able to gather the collective intelligence of employees to predict companies' performance.

The dialogue between the company and its collaborators has a large impact on internal communication. Employees are asked to forecast the performance of their company, and because of their active role in the company it is possible to forecast the number of items sold in a particular period of time or of a new product. The system extends collaboration beyond scheduled meetings and across geographical, organisational, and hierarchical boundaries. It reduces operating costs by creating more efficient and multichannel collaboration opportunities.

Are the employees acting as customers or citizens? As we will see in chapter 4 the web sentiment depicts CrowdWorx as a platform able to extend team member engagement, satisfaction and productivity. The incentive for employees appears in both economic and emotional motives.

They receive a financial reward for their contribution as well as feeling that they are an active part of the company. Predictive bets are individual, and the employee who guesses the performance closest to the actual results receives a financial incentive as well as public and collective gratification from contributing to the company's performance.

The *one-to-many* collaboration in *pre-sale activity* is present in many other cases. Mountain Dew, a carbonated soft drink brand produced and owned by PepsiCo and distributed mainly in the US, decided to crowd-source not only the conversations about the brand but also the product selection. A similar concept is accepted by the Japanese company Muji, that creates designs of furniture only if they are previously accepted by the online clientele. Other sites for product customization include Johnflue-vogshoes, Build A Bear.Com and Adidas.

In the case of Mountain Dew the collaboration goes beyond the selection of products. The homepage features short films of two products and the one consumers prefer is put into production. Superficially, the model is very simple, but there appears to be a dimension of collective transgression in membership in the 'alternative' group "We Dew". For several years, the company has sponsored the well-known world skateboard and BMX event, the "Dew tour", and most of its online comments concern emotive and sensory aspects of taking part in the challenge. Although many posts also show appreciation of the drink itself, Mountain Dew can easily be imitated and is constantly competing with rival products such as Red Bull, Monster and Dr. Pepper. So it is important that many posts point out that the drink contains high levels of sugar, caffeine and artificial colouring and is blamed by dentists for tooth decay and other problems and is thus unsuitable for young people's breakfast. Interesting comments come from parents who say they will never again give Mountain Dew to their children because it made them "jump like monkeys". There are also descriptions of the damage caused to teeth.

In other words, the community effect appears to be very strong in almost all comments, both positive or negative. This is a clear example of what we call "public scrutiny": companies who open the conversation are clearly under observation by the crowd.

The one-to-many philosophy is present also in the case of platforms based on prize contests. Cisco Systems awards large annual cash prizes for innovative ideas for business. In the same way, IBM gathers ideas and awards prizes to the best users of its technologies. A further example is the

XPrize Foundation, described by its founders as "an educational non-profit organization whose mission is to bring about radical breakthroughs for the benefit of humanity, thereby inspiring formation of new industries and revitalization of markets that are currently stuck due to existing failures or a commonly held belief that a solution is not possible". In 2010, the XPrize sponsor was Google, which supplied a cash prize for technical solutions to deliveries to the moon. In a highly publicised move, Google also offered a large financial reward for the best mobile phone platform on the market in February 2008. Netflix Prize is another example of owner sponsorship. In 2010, it awarded a prize to a group of mathematicians for a new blending algorithm, which is based on Gradient Boosted Decision Trees, which can forecast the success of TV series. In a very different sector, in 2007 *Darpa Urban Challenge* offered a $2 million prize to the team that could build a fully autonomous self-driving robotic car to navigate over 60 miles of a city-like driving environment. This one-to-many approach can be applied to very different industries with lower financial incentives. *Topcoder*, for example, offers online computer programming competitions in Java, C++, and C# twice a week where members can win from $25-$300.

In all of these examples, individuals are providing their knowledge and being rewarded with money, and the risks of exploitation appear to be lowered by the transparency of the promise.

Many-to-many Co-planning: Innocentive

Starting from the one-to-many pre-sale activities, we can shift to a new group of social conversations driven by a many-to-many logic.

The first example of *co-research* is InnoCentive, whose homepage reads "… become a solver, as a Solver, you can apply your expertise, stretch your intellectual and creative boundaries, and win cash prizes from $5,000 to $1,000,000 for solving problems in a variety of domains that run the gambit from corporate to humanitarian". The name is a conflation of the words *Innovation* and *Incentive*, and the site is heavily sponsored by the pharmaceutical industry as well as other commercial enterprises, which have made it very successful.

Clients of this "knowledge many-to-many broker" include Procter and Gamble, NASA and many others. The Economist magazine, for example, recently offered a prize of €10,000 for contributions on particular issues.

The success of InnoCentive has inspired many similar sites. Chaordix was set up for marketing research and communication, and there is also Bigideagroup, owned by WPP, one of the world's largest communications service groups.

Deal4all is a site posing common problems raised by any social media user. In the summer of 2010, the challenge of the month was to find a way of keeping beaches clean. The homepage promised only psychological gratification: "If the idea can be submitted to a company or institution that may put it to practice, be sure we will try! However, as we always point out, we cannot guarantee results for such attempts. In any case, we believe that good ideas deserve to be known. Now is your chance to participate!".

Like in the one-to-many cases, these examples show individuals who freely provide their knowledge in exchange for money, and also more. Probably they are not acting as customers, but as companies themselves.

Peer-to-peer Co-planning: City 2.0

The third category of co-planning platform is driven by a peer-to-peer philosophy. Since planning activity requires financial investment it is not very common to find a peer-to-peer activity without the direct involvement of companies. This category certainly includes many cases of crowdfunding, such as Kickstarter, Buyacredit.Com, Sellaband, Profounder and Kiva, etc. In these cases individuals can supply cash and become shareholders of start-up companies whose projects are too small for traditional financial support.

At a first glance, the collaboration is driven by economic goals, but the crowd-funded projects are always very small and we are seeing a sort of "family and friends" capitalism which reduces the distances between the market and society.

In Italy, Poste Italiane has launched the crowdfunding platform Eppela, which has financed hundreds of projects. The average value of the funded projects is less than 10,000 euro. The projects that reach 50% of the requested budget, receive the remaining 50% from Poste or other foundations.

A different way to apply the peer-to-peer model in the co-planning phase is that used by City 2.0. This is a multimedia platform linking citizens, firms, professionals and administrations in real time for the sharing of ideas and schemes for a "green city". The service is promoted by TED,

Technology Entertainment Design, a non-profit group founded in 1984 by Richard Saul Wurman and Harry Marks with the aim of promoting and sharing innovative ideas that could change the world. Its slogan is "Ideas worth spreading". At a first glance the ethical goals of the platform are not completely consistent with the membership scheme. In fact until 2006, membership was by invitation only and cost $4,400, giving members the right to take part in conferences, receive information and participate in the network. The TED Prize was instituted in 2005 with a first prize worth $100,000, and in recent years prize winners have been of very high calibre and have made valuable investments. The 2012 TED prize, however, was to award the sum of $100,000 to ten different scholarship grants for projects appearing on City 2.0 putting forward the best solutions for cities based on sustainability, energy efficiency and integrated planning.

2.   Co-production

In these co-value models the consumer is not involved in planning, but in executive or production activities.

One-to-many Co-production: Huffington Post

The first example is the User Generated Media business model, well represented by the Huffington Post, which is an infotainment blog founded in the US by Arianna Huffington, Kenneth Lerer and others in 2005.

The Huffington Post soon became one of the most visited websites in the world. It gathers information from areas such as politics, technology, current affairs and entertainment, with sections for all of these and more. For several years, it lived on news supplied by a collective of freelance journalists acting as prosumers who gained only psychological gratification and no payment. The financial mechanism is the sale of contacts, not the sale of content. Huffington Post supplies a high number of contacts, which in turn need to be ensured through the attractiveness of the content. Content is free because the costs of its maintenance and presentation are covered by the sale of contacts; the opportunity for dialogue is a tradable item.

The Huffington Post is free to consumers, as advertising space is sold to pay for design and coordination. The website displays two different versions of the headlines at the same time and after a few minutes, the one that has attracted the most visitors is chosen, in a sort of crowdsourcing mechanism.

In interpreting this and similar cases, it is important to bear in mind the underlying economic model: if the consumers themselves produce content, the producer/publisher simply has the role of establishing contacts and producing layout. Revenue comes from advertising. This is a reversal of the traditional chain of value, and raises new ideological questions. The citizen journalist reporting a news item before anyone else is clearly motivated by money and his/her action is essentially a gift to the community. The reward is only that the item will appear online fast and without charge for other users. It may seem that publishers are the main beneficiaries of this new form of value creation. A recent class action brought by Huffington Post bloggers demanded a share of the 315 million dollars earned by the sale of Huffington Post to AOL, claiming that they had contributed to bringing in readers, content and the high profile of the site.

Other examples of UGC can be found in the world of open source technologies. One of the best-known is Linux, an enormous online community of designer-fans who give their time freely on a network of well-paid experts adapting and updating management solutions. These sites have interesting theoretical implications as they involve legal issues concerning patents and profit-sharing. Programmers benefit from the trickle-down effects of consultancies and applications.

There are many similar communities. Firefox and Adobe use an open source model with the help of a thousand voluntary programmers. Smartphone apps are often derived from UGC. Apple currently hosts more than 500 I-Phone apps, designed by individual creators, that can be downloaded free of charge. The production of video-games is often based on UGC.

However, for firms there are risks as well as advantages, as shown by the recent competition run by Samsung to find 30 "Android" beta testers, referees or guides from communities to test a new generation of mobile phones. In this case, the know-how of the communities was rewarded through payment in kind; and the best referees received six new-generation phones. A dedicated Facebook group, a YouTube channel for video-reviews and a Twitter account for brief updates supported the initiative. The result was that news spread rapidly outside the firm through online "word of mouth", and if a defect were detected in the software for downloading phone applications, there would be widespread public awareness of the problem.

These examples demonstrate that the risks of the new social game affect both the parties, companies and customers.

Many-to-many Co-production: GigWalk

If we apply the model presented above to a many-to-many platform we discover new business models. Let's take the case of Gigwalk in the United States, or Roamler in the Netherlands, or Bemyeye in Italy. In these smartphone-based platforms, individuals are asked to carry out market research by taking pictures to supply useful information to firms, which are not always identified. A supermarket display or billboard may be interesting information for the trade if it comes from a particular area. The gamers can earn a small sum for a single picture and transform this activity into a job. The model is many-to-many since the platform collects many bids from many companies.

The philosophy based on co-production of information can also be applied to websites. An example is a co-research web platform like Survey-Monkey, which runs surveys in very short times and is used by numerous firms. Mob4Hire is a different community that asks its members to do beta testing of applications and games. Users register on the site, state their geographical location and the type of terminal they use, and are contacted based on the project to be tested. A more specialized type of website is Rent a Coder: "If you're looking to build a website, make a design, search for writers or any other custom work, then you are on the right website. Rent a coder offers you a huge list of freelancers who will bid on your project."

In all of these cases individuals can provide information rewarded by money. The risk of exploitation appears to be lowered by the transparency of the concept, since the bidders are clearly companies.

Peer-to-peer Co-production: Amazon Turk

The model appears a bit different when there are many bidders are many and they are citizens. This is the case of Amazon Turk, a platform which shows over 120,000 micro-tasks being offered online. The unit payment is very low, but the tasks involved can be performed at any time of the day in front of a computer. The tasks consist of tagging webpage photos or proofreading and are requested by a high number of contacts. The presence of these requesters is ensured through the attractiveness of the content.

There are many examples of this type of crowdsourcing. Websites include Peopleperhour, Guru, Connect, Shorttask and Mcent.

A slightly different case is Txteagle from New Mexico that has an added social dimension compared to the other firms; it works mainly in poor and developing countries and pays inhabitants for tasks such as translations and transcriptions of conversations and other audio files and taking part in surveys. The only technology it uses is cell phones and text messaging.

The peer-to-peer philosophy is present in many other platforms. Quora, for example, is an information social network where users can post questions and answers on any topic. So here, consumers are asking other consumers to 'produce' information and the business model is different in that the website is financed by advertising. Quora was founded in 2009 by two ex-employees of Facebook, Adam D'angelo and Charlie Cheever. On the Quora website, questions and answers are grouped by topic, and users can vote and add comments. Quora was set up because although there were already numerous question and answer websites, the founders thought that none were of satisfactory quality. On Quora, users can both ask and answer questions, as well as post comments inside questions and vote either positively or negatively on replies. The business model is based on sale of advertising space.

In all these cases the players' expectations are not only financial. As we'll see in the chapter 4, the logic of gift appears often among the drivers of the conversation.

3.   Co-advertising

A new type of co-value creation is in the area of communication.

One-to-many Co-advertising: Ducati

In this case it's very common for the promoter of the collaboration to be a single company. So we can easily find the one-to-many model well depicted by the concept of *brand communities*.

One of the best-known Italian companies that uses social levers in its brand communities is Ducati motorcycles. The CEO of Ducati often chats informally and spontaneously with motorcyclists in the Ducati web community. This is an example of co-planning thanks to the continuous feedback about the products and related services that the company receives directly from product purchasers and users (Prandelli, Sawhaney and Ve-

rona, 2009). The portal Il Mulinochevorrei.it from Barilla pasta and bis-
cuit firm works in a similar way. The Procter & Gamble homepage states
that 50% of products are developed with consumers and people outside the
company. As we have seen, Procter & Gamble uses specialized external
platforms like Innocentive to crowdsource ideas for innovation, but on its
home page invites customers to supply ideas.

If we follow the one-to-many brand communities we'll find many, var-
ied case histories. Lego drew an enormous amount of inspiration from the
online communities of architects and designers taking part in its Mind-
storm NXT. With its 500 wants you communities FIAT gathered important design ideas for cars, and Mattel, the toy manufacturer, received over
two million contacts about Barbie's new boyfriend. In 2008 Master Card,
Sky, Blue and Sony launched a competition for ideas for advertising commercials that were judged at the Cannes Film Festival. In the US, Pepsi,
Hewlett Packard, Philips, VISA and Doritos promoted creativity compe-
titions for commercials to air during the Super Bowl. Porsche launched its
Tiro Rapido project in Italy in 2009 inviting the public to write a detective
story taking place in eight Italian cities in just 550 minutes. In the same
year, Polaroid asked its communities for names of candidates for key company roles such as sales director, among other examples.

The list could go on, but the concept is clear: a brand raises its profile
and receives input for product design from dialogue with consumers.

In some cases, dialogue concerns co-generation of ideas about social
responsibility. Pepsi-Cola for example has created its 'Improve Your
World' portal where consumers can put forward and vote on ideas which
are then financed by Pepsi. The areas are somewhat ambitiously called:
"urban areas", "school/work" and "connecting". Votes are converted into
credits that are valid for a prize draw for electronic gadgets.

In all these cases it is clear that companies are investing in a new form of
communication – *information as output* – but at the same time are actually
acquiring new content and advice free of charge – *information as input*. Consequently, the original debate about the risk of exploitation remains open.

Many-to-many Co-advertising: Zoopa

The interaction model changes when the platform collects many bids and
many co-advertising offers. This is the case of a platform such as Zoopa,
which offers creative contests with prizes that can reach up to 20,000 euro.

2 Consumption implies work

Firms which have used Zoopa recently include Auchan, Nike, Google, Pago and many others. Sites like Crowdspring, Ideabounty, and Userfarm are similar. Each aims for a particular field; Boblr, for example, features design, and Voices.com asks for voices for commercials, voice-overs and videos etc.

In all these cases the risk of exploitation is lowered by the transparency of the concept: money for ideas. Individuals are taking part in the game as neither customers nor citizens, but rather as freelance professionals.

The platforms aimed at managing bloggers conversations appear to be less transparent. Let's take the example of Klout, a platform which calls itself the most advanced online social rating service and the benchmark for measuring social networks.

Its homepage reads: "Discover and be recognized for how you influence the world". So, there is an almost explicit mention of co-advertising, and users put their reputation up for sale. Klout uses a secret algorithm to incorporate more than 400 signals from seven different networks, including Mentions, Likes, Comments, Subscribers, Wall Posts and Friends. The Klout Score ranges from 1 to 100, the maximum influence. Klout Style is also interesting. It provides an assessment of users' influence on style or personality. The site reads: "How often do you share links or directly engage with others? Do you tend to share or create original content? The style is shown graphically and thus reveals what about the user interests the networks the most, and what doesn't. This is where the activity becomes explicitly commercial: "Be Rewarded! Klout Perks are exclusive products or experiences that you earn based on your influence. Influencers have earned sweet Perks like laptops and airline tickets. Perks are available to everyone, not just people with high scores. We care about the topics that you're interested and influential in. You have no obligation to talk about the product. You're welcome to tell the world you love it, you dislike it, or say nothing at all".

A Klout score can actually bring big perks in money and savings. There are already hotels in the US, such as the Palms Casino Resort in Las Vegas, which offer discounts to customers with a high score. Chevrolet recently launched an advertising campaign with Klout in the US whereby high scorers could use the Chevrolet Volt for a weekend, as a perk, in the hope that they would raise the profile of the brand. Klout is used by 100 million people, and until recently carried only personal profiles. But today Klout Brand Squad applies the system directly to brands to measure their influence and reputation.

This last case is very interesting, since it reinforces the theoretical risks of exploitation. In fact, the paid Klout bloggers can actually manipulate crowd feeling through company pressure.

Peer-to-peer Co-advertising: Pinterest

We are now in the field of classic social platforms like Facebook or Twitter. Among these, one of particular interest is Pinterest. The name Pinterest is a conflation of 'pinboard' and 'interest'. Pinterest is a social network for sharing photos and images, based on the idea of a big online pinboard, where users can 'hang' their interests and create and update collections of images. Most of these concern purchase and consumption, so conversations often comprise post-sale conversations where citizens discuss concrete goods, rather than services, in the role of consumers. *Pinterest* is one of the 100 most visited websites in the world. Pinboard is currently the eighth largest social network in the world, carrying 3% of total online traffic. The main use is for sharing interests, and therefore ideas. Pinterest has recently been taken over by Facebook, so there may be new developments coming in the use of advertising on the site.

Users create a flow of posts on a topic that can either be chosen from a list or introduced ad hoc. The more unusual the topic, the more successful it is likely to be. The new 'note' is categorized on the site and displayed on the pinboard for that topic along with other users' posts. As on Facebook, you can 'Like' other users' posts, and as on Twitter, you can Repin, or re-post someone else's content on your own pinboard. The aim of Pinterest is to connect people with topics they are interested in and inspired by. It is extremely user-friendly and using images means communication is effective, powerful and fast.

4.   Co-selling

The conversation takes new form when its contents are related to the sale process.

One-to-many Co-selling: Threadless

The first example is Threadless, a platform promoted by one company aimed at obtaining many inputs from many customers. The platform produces customizable t-shirts. Launched in 2000 and based in Chicago, the brand uses the classic T-shirt as its canvas, creating a line of one-of-a-kind pieces that are produced in limited runs. From slogan and graphics, to abstract and photography prints, Threadless uses the most popular designs as voted on by its online community to adorn its coveted tops. In this case customers act as designers. They are repaid through money and gift value. In fact a t-shirt sold produces a royalty for the author, but also the satisfaction of being considered an artist or a fashion designer. In this case, co-advertising is integrated with co-selling, and clients provide inputs for production as well as talking about products.

Other websites have been set up along the same lines as Threadless. These include JPGmag, the prestigious photography magazine, which selects photographs from those offered by online communities and pays 100 dollars per photo for the best. It deals with 30,000 photographs a month and prints the same number of copies, although high costs are currently endangering the business model. This is based on sales of advertising contacts, so that a high number of fans, who are also users, are necessary for the site to succeed.

Many-to-many Co-selling: Ebay

The most famous case of many-to-many co-selling is of course eBay, a website which holds some surprises when looked at more closely. The eBay site is a marketplace allowing users to buy and sell new and used items at any time and from any computer online. Sales can be 'online auctions' or at a fixed price. In many cases sellers are professionals, and this is the reason why eBay cannot be considered a peer-to-peer platform.

There are various sales formats; standard, reserve and multiple item auctions, fixed-price 'Buy It Now', and mixed auction/fixed price. Professional and amateur sellers offer goods or services and buyers bid for them. As we'll see, user comments reveal a big psychological component in buying and selling. Many refer to the emotional aspect of bidding, although obviously the model is entirely based on economics, buying, and selling. eBay is widely held to be reliable and only a few comments call its reputation into question. Consumer inputs show a clear peer-to-peer dimension. Comments usually focus on behaviour of other users, ranging from collaboration and putting up goods for sale, to payments, delivery and customer care aspects, rather than how the site works. Given that it is driven by strong individual motivation, overall eBay is a clear metaphor for the way that society and market converge and money and gifts can work together.

A different architecture of value is the one promoted by Groupon, an example of a purchasing group. The coupon model gives an active role to the consumer who involves friends and acquaintances in buying minimum amounts of products.

Andrew Mason founded Groupon in the US in 2008. The name is a conflation of 'Group' and 'Coupon'. Groupon has become synonymous with social shopping all over the world. It opened in Italy in 2010 and rapidly spread all over the country. The "Citydeal" slogan is clear and makes an explicit reference to where coupon promotions are taking place. The business model is simple: the infomediary offers local retailers, restaurants etc. the chance to give e-Coupons to consumers. The consumer is attracted by savings and shares interests with friends and acquaintances. Collective purchasing power allows Groupon to cut prices of quality goods and services much more than other operators.

In both cases, eBay and Groupon, the financial model appear to be transparent and the theoretical risk of exploitation is not substantial.

A different solution for many-to-many co-selling is the service Facebook provides which shows your friends all your past Facebook Places check-ins and recent check-ins from your friends. You can also click on a friend or place and view the full check-in history. In this case companies can invite customers to check in to a restaurant or a hotel with your friends and consequently get rewards or discounts.

In this case as well the reward scheme is transparent, but the privacy issue is much more relevant than in the previous cases.

Peer-to-peer Co-selling: Fab

A new example of a co-selling platform is Fab, an online community of creative designers which is a virtual marketplace for individuals' output. Fab represents a cross between co-advertising and co-selling, since one of the goals is sales.

Fab, originally called Fabulis, was founded in February 2010 by Jason Goldberg, a veteran of design production, and Bradford Shellhammer. In two years, it achieved remarkable success in the US, and since 2011 has rapidly become popular in Europe, especially in Germany, the Netherlands and France, as well as Eastern Asian countries like China and Japan.

Many American companies have invested in it. In December 2011, Fab. com obtained 40 million dollars from the Andreessen Horowitz venture capital firm, on top of 8 million dollars from Menlo Ventures in July of the same year. Fab's main innovations include the "live Feed" which gives consumers the chance to tell others what they are buying and share their reactions and emotions using Fab.com tweets.

Social and relational aspects tend to override the financial side. It is very close to social commerce, which is becoming increasingly widespread, such as Rakuten for Japanese products and Wishpot for children and wedding gift lists.

5. Co-logistics

A new type of value co-creation is in the area of logistics.

One-to-many Co-logistics: Enjoy

The first solution is represented by the classic car sharing services like Enjoy in Italy or ZipCar or Car2Go in US. The benefit is to drive a car without owning one.

The company is the owner of the cars and the transaction is one-to-many. The spots where users pick up or park the cars are easy to find around the city and the mobile app gives the customers a great picture of where cars are available. Customers can reserve a car online or from the convenience of their mobile device. They don't have to worry about paying for gas either. Companies provide a gas card in each vehicle in addition to insurance coverage on each vehicle and 24/7 roadside assistance.

Many-to-many Co-logistics: Deliveroo

The model changes when the platform connects suppliers and buyers of logistics services. This is the case of Uber, but also new home delivery platforms like Just Eat, Deliveroo or Supermercato 24. In these cases we see a many-to-many architecture. Customers must simply enter their postal code to find a local restaurant or supermarket that delivers food to their home. The service is not guaranteed by a private network of vehicles and drivers but is outsourced to the crowd. Obviously the citizens who wish to drive from restaurants to homes and offices need to respect some service standards.

Apparently this model doesn't produce any risk of exploitation. Nevertheless, many journalistic discussions have arisen, since the payments of drivers or bikers are very low and the forms of employment are clearly temporary.

Peer-to-peer Co-logistics: Waze

The last model of co-logistics is peer-to-peer. An interesting case is that of Waze. The home page of this platform reads: "Imagine millions of drivers out on the roads, working together towards a common goal: to outsmart traffic and get everyone the best route to work and back, every day".

Waze is the world's largest community-based traffic and navigation app. Drivers can join other drivers in their area and share real-time traffic and road info, saving everyone time and fuel on their daily commute. Their claim is "Nothing can beat real people working together".

The concept is very simple and the economic model is explained by the capability of the platform to collect and resell info about drivers' behaviour. For example, an advertising billboard or the new opening of a store can clearly benefit of this info. For now the app doesn't contain brand advertising.

6.   Co-use

A new model of collaboration is linked to the final stage of usage of products and services.

One-to-many Co-use: World of Warcraft

Some of the best-known co-use platforms are related to the world of games. World of Warcraft was developed by Blizzard Entertainment, and the first version appeared on November 23, 2004. It became the most popular game of its type in the world and tens of millions registered online to play. The success was a surprise to its creators, who before it was launched had said they would consider it successful if they sold one million games.

The website is clearly also in the business of co-advertising and co-selling where the consumer provides a service to the firm. There exists a parallel market in the sale of points and characters that shows a form of community self-government inspired by the market.

Co-gaming is found on many other web sites. Xbox Live is the Microsoft portal for videogames and online gamers. It can be accessed only by payment and the 23 million video gamers around the world can play online, chat, send and receive messages, and so on. Xbox Live thus allows for maximum interaction between users in gaming and interpersonal communication.

Many-to-many Co-use: Kahn Academy

The many-to-many logic appears again in platforms which make it possible to use a service simultaneously for many suppliers and many users. This is the case of platforms for sharing digital contents. For example, the Kahn Academy is a very well-known example of a co-use website where the consumer can make themself known for their knowledge and ability to train other people. The mission of the platform is to enable access to free world-class education for anyone anywhere.

A similar many-to-many service is SlideShare, which contains many academic research papers provided by private and public institutions. In both cases the philosophy is the same of Wikipedia, but the contents are provided also by companies. Linkedin also does this, helping citizens and companies to get in touch and co-use their private information.

Peer-to-peer Co-use: Nextdoor

A third category of co-use is connected to the sharing of physical space. This is the case of *Nextdoor*, which promotes co-use in car sharing, road sharing and other similar schemes. Nextdoor is a free online platform that enables neighbours to create private social networks for their neighbourhood. They can communicate with one another to build stronger and safer neighbourhoods.

The concept is simple, as is its slogan: "Join the free private social network for your neighbourhood". Its homepage reads: "Over 4,000 communities across the U.S. are using Nextdoor to strengthen their neighbourhoods. We believe that the neighbourhood is one of the most important and useful communities in a person's life. We believe that when neighbours start talking, good things happen. Our mission is to bring back a sense of community to the neighbourhood".

There is a long list of possible types of collaboration. People use Nextdoor to track down trustworthy babysitters, plumbers, and dentists; get the word out about break-ins and other safety concerns; organize neighbourhood garage sales, BBQs, and block parties; ask for assistance in finding lost pets and missing packages and to create emergency response plans to prepare for crisis situations.

As we have mentioned, this is the same philosophy behind BlaBlaCar and Airbnb, to which chapter 5 is dedicated.

7.   Co-post use

The last phase of collaboration takes place after consumption.

One-to-many Co-post use: Nintendo

In many industries it is normal to encourage customers to contribute to service reviews. Nintendo usually tests its Gameboy beta versions on its customers; Stargate fans may agree to translate the subtitles of films into local languages, and so on. The psychological gratification is strengthened by the final physical output of co-creation. Nevertheless, the risk for a complete disclosure of product defects can be very high.

Many-to-many Co-post use: TripAdvisor

The most famous platform of many-to-many post use is surely TripAdvisor. Its concept is not different from the service rating offered by sites such as Digg and Delicious. As we'll see in chapter 4, TripAdvisor is overused by companies and in many cases the risk of informational asymmetries between companies and customers doesn't disappear.

Peer-to-peer Co-post use: Zoes

In the area of peer-to-peer we find many platforms inspired by the principle of gifting. This is the case of Ifwerantheworld, Ushahidi, Cure Together, Sheilas' Wheels and many others. In the Italian market an interesting example is *Zoes*, a third sector initiative based on voluntary contributions but financed by a network of foundations and firms from the market. It is true that from an economic standpoint these organisations function on societal and gift mechanisms, but it is equally useful to recognise that they need help from the private sector. In this context it's interesting to observe platforms which act in conflict with companies.

This is the case of The Pirate Bay and all websites for illegal downloading of files. Pirate Bay is a Swedish website founded in 2003 that hosts multimedia files, videogames and Torrent. BitTorrent is a protocol that underpins the practice of peer-to-peer file sharing and is used for distributing large amounts of data over the Internet. BitTorrent is one of the most common protocols for transferring large files and it has been estimated that, collectively, peer-to-peer networks have accounted for approximately 43% to 70% of all Internet traffic.

Having fought off many legal challenges, The Pirate Bay has been called 'the most resistant site in the galaxy'. It is estimated to have 5 million users, and 3.5 million files have been downloaded. Damages to the record, film and videogames industry are estimated to exceed 110 million euro.

This business model is based on advertising, donations from wealthy individuals and the sale of gadgets. Users show that they are aware of posing a challenge to the market. While reading the comments on the web we found the following:

> Dear friends. i need help. Who knows how to download Microsoft office for free, forever. I'm trying on pirate bay, but just keep getting scripted files that aren't anything. what am i doing wrong. I just want free Microsoft word. my journaling/diary entries are waaay past due, etc…The only pirates i know are the ones in suits running banks. These guys are brilliant and i use this, saves the public money. Hard times are hitting us so these guys are saving us roughly 50 quid a month for me:) etc. You don't need The Pirate Bay to access illegal files on internet. You can just use...google. So should Google close down too??? If users supply content and the site shows where this illicit content can be accessed, who is guilty? The search engine?

Fortunately there are also comments from users who criticise pirating.

> I am shocked and disgusted by the percentage of people posting here that think downloading copyright content that they have not paid for is ok. People should grow up and develop a respect for other peoples property. and yes these movie companies and game houses do make millions, but they put in the work to get the reward.

Overall, users know that peer-to-peer sharing of illegal files underpins the website, and it is precisely the illicit nature of piracy that seems to interest them. The website itself built up the idea of challenging order and even constructed flying robots to get around legislation of particular countries. One of the many challenges they pose to the establishment is to move from digital to physical piracy:

> The digital era has made everything easier and now it is time to take the next step. As well as cultural products like books, music and films, which are created digitally, everyday objects, are also designed using software. We have decided to launch a type of file called Physibles, which will produce real objects using the right hardware. In the near future, individuals will be able to produce spare parts for their cars themselves. In twenty years' time, you will be able to download your own trainers.

Conceptually, this post shows how far the concept of community may extend. It is noticeable that there are many anti-brand communities, which help consumers to challenge the market, too. Many of these bring out the opportunities and the risks inherent in the new social game.

3 "A coke is a coke"

The ideological debate

During the industrial revolution, factories were the symbol of exploitation and the separation between capital and labour. Mass consumption, symbolized by Coca Cola, represented the answer to this ideological debate.

> *A Coke is a Coke and no amount of money can get you a better Coke than the one the bum on the corner is drinking*
>
> Andy Warhol, 1975.

But did the paradox of the Coke democracy reduce the distance between capital and labour? And today, after two centuries of conflict between *market and society* can we replace the Coca Cola society with Uber society, or Airbnb or BlaBlaCar societies? How are the new symbols of the sharing economy impacting the ideological debate?

1.   The new perspective

In the first chapter, we introduced this dichotomy:

customers = money = market = sale

vs.

citizens = gift = society = dialogue

We now look in more depth at the dichotomy between *homo civis* and *homo oeconomicus*. This new ideological and theoretical perspective (Figure 1) can be summarized in three points:

1. *Coincidence*: market and society coincide and sharing platforms or communities are the new symbol of the coincidence of *homo civis* and *homo oeconomicus*.
2. *Divergence*: market and society are in conflict and sharing platforms or communities are social entities able to develop antibodies against the market.
3. *Convergence:* market and society do not coincide but may converge towards common interests in the space belonging to sharing platform communities.

Let us look at this in more detail.

Figure 1   Ideological Perspective

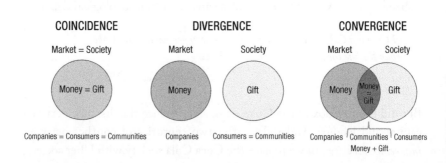

COINCIDENCE	DIVERGENCE		CONVERGENCE	
Market = Society	Market	Society	Market	Society
Money = Gift	Money	Gift	Money	Money = Gift
Companies = Consumers = Communities	Companies	Consumers = Communities	Companies	Communities	Consumers
				Money + Gift

2.   Coincidence

The optimistic vision of *coincidence* is based on the liberal axiom that market and society interests tend to coincide. This perspective was introduced by Adam Smith of course, and was implicit in his attempt to dignify the selfishness of the butcher with the "invisible hand".

In today's context, this means that the sharing economy can be seen at the same time as an expression of society, and an expression of the market, given that these are one and the same. From this perceptive, sharing platforms and peer-to-peer communities are two forms of the same model: money and gift cannot be divided.

The marketing perspective

From a marketing perspective, Evert Gummesson, before others, suggested the idea of a "value-creation network society" which implies a science or discipline with a "new foundation, new values, new assumptions or new methods" (Gummesson, 2002). In 2008, an important issue of the European Journal of Marketing was entitled *Bridging the divide* (vol. 36, n. 3) and focused on new opportunities for cooperation between companies and customers. If the consumer is also the producer – *prosumerism* – the border between market and society is blurred. In this context, radical communities can be interpreted as new common spaces where there is no longer a distinction between "peer-to-peer dialogue" based on a gift logic and "firm-consumer dialogue" based on money. Money and gift are two faces of the same coin – *homo civis* and *homo oecomomicus*. Many authors find that the new collective intelligence is imprinting new business models and creating new value.

Following this perspective, in 2002, Gummesson put forward the idea of a "value-creation network society" which implies a science or discipline with "new foundation, new values, new assumptions or new methods". Some years later, as the concept of co-creation evolved, Gummesson (2011) suggested substituting the old B2B (Business to Business) or B2C (Business to Consumers) acronyms with A2A (Actors to Actors). In this way, the divide between companies and consumers disappears, highlighting their equal role in the creation of value. Business and consumers interact closely in many-to-many networks and contribute to the creation of value.

The idea that consumer and company interests coincide appears frequently in mainstream marketing literature. In 2004, Lusch and Vargo proposed their Service Dominant Logic model in which the consumer is always the protagonist in creating value. In 2006, they wrote: "The purpose of the corporation, we argue, is to provide a mechanism for man to exchange service(s) for service(s) in order to improve his standard of living..."[1].

In 2008, Grönroos stated that "...accepting value in use as a foundational value creation concept, customers are the value creators (...) the supplier can become a co-creator of value with its customers".

---

[1] Numerous writers have linked the work of Lusch and Vargo to the ethical dimension. The most recent are Abela and Murphy (2008) and Choi (2009) who derives a new approach to business ethics from the service-dominant logic of marketing.

Many authors agree that the new forms of interaction require a new theoretical framework. Ballantyne and Varey (2008), for example analysed the new value process in which firms and consumers cooperate in the value proposition. Value is interactively co-created by companies and consumers, rather than merely exchanged (Leavy, 2004).

Perrini et al. (2007) and Von Friedrichs (2009), develop the idea of a new "Social Entrepreneurship" which they identify in new firms acting in the interests of society using traditional business models. In 2009, Schau, Muñiz and Arnould reviewed 52 articles from international marketing reviews: all of them explicitly claim to examine collective consumer behaviour and its positive implications for the market.

The industrial perspective

The positive consequences of the new revolution are also clearly described by researchers adopting different perspectives. Some describe the revolution through the more general lens of a *knowledge-based economy* (Thurow, 1997; Varian, 2001; Ancarani and Costabile, 2005). Their work shows that the new competition in knowledge is increasing collaboration and conflict between firms and is leading to a new technological convergence between sectors. In fact, when technology is no longer deterministic, as in heavy industry, the concept of industry becomes weaker as differences between markets are eroded (Rosemberg, 1976; Rispoli, 1998; Valdani, Ancari and Castaldo, 2001). In many cases, the very categorization of goods and services is called into question[2]. Indeed some industries are being completely revolutionised by customers' work; examples are music, media, information technology, finance, retailing, gaming, entertainment, tourism, and so on. In this scenario, service innovations are rarely R&D based; they are often market or customer-based (Sundbo, 1996).

In this perspective, "transactional innovation" is of equal value or higher value than "technological innovation". Relationships are in fact the ve-

---

[2] For example it's necessary to review the attributes of goods and services which were traditionally categorised as: *search qualities* – fully evaluated prior to purchase by simple inspection; *experience qualities* – evaluated only after purchase and consumption; *credence qualities* – typically taken on trust, even after search and experience, because they cannot be objectively pre-evaluated or post-evaluated by the purchaser (Nelson, 1970; Zeithaml and Bitner, 2003).

hicles that process, codify and negotiate information and raise the cognitive specialization of institutions (Snehota and Tunisini, 1999; Costabile, 2001). The consequences are positive as the relationship between the knowledge revolution – measured through the growth of information technology – and national economic performance is widely identified (McKinsey, 2011; Daveri, 2001).

The perspective of sociology

In this context, numerous ideas from sociology can be of assistance regarding human motivation and economic organization. The sociologist Manuel Castells (2008), for example, describes the "network-society", a new morphology where technology and society coincide. This coincidence implies a publicisation of the private, or a privatization of the social sphere, which shifts the boundary between the individual and society, as well as between society and market. The concept of "corporation citizenship" enters the marketing dictionary to describe a company's role in, or responsibilities towards, society. The change is influencing anthropological and epistemological research. Yochai Benkler (2006) describes a "Wealth of Networks", a network of people who cooperate to reach social ideals with the aim of setting up a company but without any remuneration.

Norbert Elias (2000) describes the shift from a society of individuals to a network of relationships based on cooperation. Many economists note that the influence between public and private interests is still today at the core of financial performance.

George Akerlof and Robert Shiller (2009), for example, stress that individuals are often guided by non-financial motivation and that a sudden decline in trust is at the core of the current recession. Rachel Kranton and George Akerlof (2009) and Tore Ellingsen (2009) focus on the role of identity and social networks in the economy.

The perspective of psychology

Studies in psychology on citizen addiction to the web are raising new issues. The risk of dependence on the Internet as a pathology is briefly discussed below; but some authors find that the learning experience of being a digital customer and citizen at the same time strengthens the individual process of self-identity building, so that conversations about brands are not really dangerous. Many years ago, in 1986, Sproul and Kiesler pointed out that language on the web carries no social cues, so that in front of a computer we are all "de-individualized" and therefore equal. Many writers today say that the Internet is speeding up learning processes and disseminating a standardized common language of signs and symbols globally, which offers significant opportunities for individual and collective knowledge. If it is true that imitation and physical experience are the basis for learning, the new social media offer a wealth of opportunities. It is similar to how TV once boosted literacy and the creation of shared social norms. There is a great deal of literature on how social-identity creation, norms and culture affect market success in contexts similar and different from western culture (Kranton and Akerlof, 2009). The new role of the collectivity is to mediate the complexity of information and heuristically convert it into a new codified knowledge. For some writers, these new languages are making citizens more trustworthy and open to dialogue and are helping to bring about a new collective intelligence (Olleros, 2008; Mathwick, Wiertz and de Ruyter, 2008). Recently, Pier Levy (2008) claimed that the virtual world constitutes a strengthening of reality rather than an escape.

Many writers claim that brands can comprise a shared cultural property, something belonging to all of us. From this perspective, goods and services become "conversations" (Barthes, 1987) and fashions and norms become metaphors for living together to be decoded through narrative psychology. "Talking about your consumption habits means recognizing yourself" (Franchi, 2007). Market and society conversations tend to overlap and to be continuous. Because goods and services have a symbolic value, using them involves the individual in relating to others and speeds up social processes connected to learning (Moriggi and Nicoletti, 2009).

Early work in this field was done by Holbrook and Hirschman (1992); Nunnally and Bernstein (1999); Schmitt (1999, 2003) and Abruzzese and Ferraresi (2009). All these authors agree that the new sensitivity to words, images and music needs to be considered as a new opportunity for society. The principle of the importance of beauty current in the Renaissance and Bauhaus is still valid today. Art and creativity are important interfaces between society and market, and beauty can represent a form of knowledge and research. Aesthetics is an important form of knowledge and socialization and its potential is increased by new forms of dialogue (Senadi, 2009;

Zeki, 2007)[3]. In this scenario, semiotic literature suggests new spaces for textual cooperation which leads to a sort of "aestheticization" of life (Featherstone, 1991; Goffman, 1969).

The ethics perspective

More generally, there is a great deal of literature on the new trust mechanisms which are said to be leading to new social responsibility. Kollock (1998) describes the concepts of reciprocity and reputation which are increasing the sense of efficacy and attachment. Belk (2010) focuses on the concept of "sharing", as a fundamental consumer behaviour that is different from commodity exchange and gift giving (Bergquist and Ljiungberg, 2001).

One recent study by Mathwick, Wiertz and de Ruyter (2008) focuses on the influence of relational norms on social capital in a virtual community where voluntarism, reciprocity, and social trust play important roles. In the new context, respect for the environment and social sensitivity are the key to success for firms aiming to profit in new areas. It could be argued that commercial exploitation of ethical behaviour by companies is in no way reprehensible, given that market interests coincide with society's. Although the behaviour is market driven, the effects on society are positive and important. But this view shows a cynicism typical of economists, and we need a more thorough interpretation of prosumerism before we can adopt what is in fact a more optimistic interpretation.

3.   Divergence

Despite the over-optimism of the service-marketing mainstream, many authors suggest caution. This ideological aversion to the classic paradigm of economic literature is introduced as a consequence of the new value

---

[3] Experience has been discussed as an expression of hedonism (e.g. Hirschman and Holbrook 1982, Campbell, 2005) Campbell describes the craft consumer; Jon Sundbo (2009) focuses on expressive consumption which becomes increasingly less instrumental and more expressive. According to Derrida the "collage" is the main shape of post-modern language; according to Fabris (2009), surfing the net with boredom is similar to the random walks taken by Baudelaire's flaneur. Semprini suggests that the society of the "flow" is leading to new forms of involuntary knowledge, a sort of serendipity.

creation model. Prosumption is more than an economic activity (Holt, 1995; Xie, Bagozzi and Troye, 2008; Firat, 1991), so, the theoretical debate requires a multidisciplinary approach.

The new Big Brother

Castells describes a sort of meta-market as the result of privatization of public spaces or publicisation of private spaces. He underlines the risk that the consumer can no longer distinguish between public and private spaces. Orwell's *Big Brother* (Animal Farm, 1943) inevitably comes to mind. Galimberti (1999), referring to Heidegger, points out that *man becomes a machine* and, as the rhythms of man are not the same as the rhythms of a machine, acceleration is dangerous. The goals of the economy are not the same as the goals of mankind. Braudillard (2005) wrote "The history of the representation of the world appears to have reached its end, the world is disappearing. If everything is information, nothing really informs us"[4].

Pessimism also permeates the work of Paul Virilio on the information bomb, and the work of post-modern thinkers such as Vattimo who describes the end of modernity and the concept of truth, thus legitimizing a relativism that is on the threshold of nihilism (Virilio, 1994; Vattimo, 1984).

Concerns about economic exploitation are of course reflected in concerns about society as a whole. In 2000, Rifkin put forward a charismatic view of a fusion of society and market, of life and labour: "Our society is increasingly close to a world without workers".

In this way the current conflict between capital and labour differs clearly from the conflict occurring during the industrial revolution. Intangible labour involves all members of society, it is a sort of *living labour*, based on cultural foundations of trade in goods and services.

---

[4] Baudrillard (2005) writes "This absence of reality, the physicality of the word surrounding us reveals a significant mechanism linked to vision: we no longer look at things; it is things that look at us. The world we live in is a hyper-reality made up of sign-objects". A recent survey of the Italian market by GPK measured the number of individual contacts made by an old-fashioned consumer compared to a digital consumer of working age. On a typical day, the old-fashioned consumer meets 9.2 people at home, meeting places and shops, and speaks to 3.9 people. The modern digital consumer on average meets over 20 people at home and work, sends 9 text messages, 11.7 emails, 3.8 instant messages, 7.7 telephone calls and has 36.8 social networking contacts. Superficially, this may seem positive, but there of course is a worrying downside, as the desire to socialize leads to a decline in real world contact.

Negri, in fact, asks, "Why should the act of living not receive a wage to take account of the fact that each person, simply because she lives in a productive society, is productive in him/herself"[5]? Recent research has indeed tried to calculate the enormous contribution made by housewives, the unemployed and pensioners to the common good (Burda, 2009)[6].

The new addiction

Economic psychology is currently voicing some of the same concerns as philosophy, and the risk of market logic overcoming all others is encapsulated in the title of an Italian book *Felici e sfruttati* or "Happy and Exploited" (Formenti, 2010). In fact, if economic exploitation were reinforced by a hedonistic and addictive experience it would be a dangerous thing. This same idea that market can defeat man can be seen in man's psychological dependence on technology.

McLuhan's concerns regarding TV, that the medium is the message, are even more current now; interest is focused on the container rather than on content. If the container is an interactive machine, like a computer or a smartphone, then man can only become more heavily addicted. The existence of this risk is confirmed by a new area of research which is shedding light on the experiential and social functioning of our brain (Weber, 2007; Dalli, 2004; Motterlini, 2005; Gallese, 2008; Zeki, 2007; Lugli, 2009).

These researchers find that imitation and physical experience are the basis for learning[7]. They are what drives the identity building processes and influence the individual's desire for recognition. Thanks to the digital revolution, learning processes are taking on new forms and the exploitation of images and texts is bringing new languages into existence. This

---

[5] Interview with Espresso 10/02/09.

[6] A recent survey by the Chamber of Commerce of Milan shows that savings achieved from work carried out at home by grandparents amount to about nine billion euro in the region of Lombardy. Research on unemployment shows that the unemployed make a large contribution to work in society (Burda, 2009). Much recent economic research focuses on social issues (Kranton and Akerkof, 2009, Ellingsten, 2009).

[7] It appears that certain areas of the brain are activated by the sight of others performing an action, and those important mechanisms of imitation are stimulated by mirror neurons. The motor cortex in the brain activates spontaneously and unconsciously when stimulated by seeing actions previously encoded in deep memory. This activation mechanism also occurs through hearing phrases describing the action as well as listening to music that reawakens memories.

stimulation is activated instantaneously, and communicated by signals linked to previous experiences relating to an implicit memory not accessible by conscious thought. This is a sort of biological *ego* very different from rational awareness, and many writers have linked it to the working of the immune system (Petre, 2003).

It is in fact in the area of experiencing that new technologies have proved most surprising, and for this reason most dangerous. Empirical studies provide interesting results; the Internet may have a higher level of noise and redundancy of message than TV, and spamming is particularly bothersome, but its interactive nature activates mental algorithms that over time increase the efficacy of the relationship. The use of words, images and music combined with its interactive nature creates an unprecedented potential for involvement.

This of course is important for our understanding of psychological consequences of digital conversations, which are often not mediated by rationality and which can lead to new types of pathologies. The following researchers focus on the negative effects of the new mind-set.

Carr (2008) and Greenfield (2000) collect empirical evidence of new weaknesses in higher-order cognitive processes, including abstract vocabulary, mindfulness, reflection, inductive problem solving, critical thinking, and imagination. They warn against serious repercussions such as psychological dependence on the Internet. The urgent need for research into online adolescent information searching has often been expressed (La Ferle et al., 2000; Fisoun et al., 2012). This clinical concern leads to a scientific debate that has not yet been resolved and has many ideological implications.

The risk of exploitation

Regarding these concerns, many economists believe that the cynicism of the profit-dominant philosophy or the "amoral paradigm" which arose with industrialization can be abandoned. In the 1970s Milton Friedman and other economists, following Adam Smith, claimed that economics is, and ought to be, a value-free science, devoid of ethical considerations.

However, Freeman (1994) described this 'Separation Thesis' as dangerous, although it is prevalent in contemporary business thought, since ethical issues cannot be clearly separated from business issues. Following Freeman (1994), Shepard, Wimbush and Stephens (1995) and Abela

(2001) suggest that market and society goals should not be separated. According to Abela (2001) "ethical approaches will be marginalized as long as the separation thesis prevails."

In our first chapter, we introduced the perspective of Bowen (1986, 1990) Humphreys and Grayson (2008), and others. They suggest that "it is one thing to leave assembly and transport to the customer, in return for a substantial cost advantage, like Ikea; but another thing to use the consumer's knowledge and give no cost advantage". Following Bowen's original criticism, many researchers have emphasized the risk of exploitation (Kelley, Donnelly and Skinner, 1990; Faranda, 1994; Brodie et al., 1997: Ballantyne and Varey 2008; Humphreys and Grayson, 2008). Many see a difference between "co-creation of value" and "co-production": the digital consumer in fact makes an intellectual rather than a physical contribution. Others see the customer as a "partial employee" of the service provider (Mills and Morris, 1986; Bowen and Schneider, 1988; Bateson, 1983; Keh and Teo, 2001) or as a "human resource" at its disposal (Bowen, 1986; Kelley, Skinner and Donnelly, 1992; Zeithaml and Bitner, 2003). These researchers claim that exploitation no longer takes place in factories but is moving into the home, where individuals generate production but are not rewarded by the distribution of the value they have created.

The countervailing power of Communities

In the early 1990s, Gerken noted that it is the Internet which "separates dialogue from sales" (Gerken, 1994). The new continuity of conversation – *before, during and after sale* – is found to strengthen voice, or what Hirschman called the consumer's faculty for expression (Hirschman, 1980).

On an optimistic note, Cova and Dalli (2009) appear to give new credit to the extreme points of view of Negri, who goes beyond the concept of mass and individual in his discussion of "multitudes" and new social spaces. In daily life, individuals are already ceding ground to suppliers, and sale is already taking place, but there is a ray of hope.

On the Internet there appears to be numerous cases where consumers "contribute to the social construction of reality and in return receive cultural, symbolic and affective advantages" (Cova and Dalli, 2009); although any financial benefit goes entirely to the firm (Dujarier, 2009; Salmon, 2008).

There is thus a hope that the ethical conscience of online communities can grow independently of the market. Post-Maussian theory in fact sees immaterial work as a "gift" or non-monetary exchange at a primary level of society (Grasselli and Montesi, 2009). In order to capture this gift logic, Cova describes online communities as a meta-market driven by a non-contractual innovation and inspired by linking value and aiming to defend society (Cova, 1997).

They deny that a theoretical revolution is taking place and entitle their work: "Working customers: the next step in marketing theory?" They write: "...the divide between consumers and producers remains unchanged, and contrary to post-modern visions, could be even wider...". They ask whether citizens can be protected from the risk of exploitation. Their point of view is that market and society interests cannot converge, and divergence of interests is harmful because institutions are not capable of defending citizens from exploitation. In light of these risks they ask whether peer-to-peer dialogue in online communities can be considered as an entity in itself, separate from the market[8].

Starting from the concept of *countervailing power*, other authors open new perspectives. In 2006, Arnould, Price and Malshe wrote "consumer groups have a greater voice in the co-creation of value... and exhibit a sense of moral responsibility". In practice, individuals take part in peer-to-peer conversations with a mixture of narcissism and altruism in order to feel they belong to a community, gain recognition and continue their process of identity building.

More recently, Chia (2012) has analysed how advertising is one of the most important elements of discussion between people, and how exposure to advertising influences their interaction. Many authors demonstrate that individuals' conversations are strongly influenced by the social desire to share personal experiences, knowledge and opinions about whom they interact with, in other words, companies or brands. Conversations are often based on the perception that "...there are things that the firm cannot tell you" (Firat, Dholakia and Venkatesh, 2005). The phenomenon of exploitation is sometimes a feeling, "a social construct dangerous for firms" and as such can feed on collective suggestion. Increasingly, through blogs, forums and others web

---

[8] Cova and Dalli (2009) identify at least eight strands of customer-centric thought current in recent years. A brief note also states the important roles of one part of relationship marketing (Hakansson, 1982) and consumer creativity literature (Hirschman, 1980). The first customer-centric studies in fact appeared just before or in the 1980s (Chase, 1978; Toffler, 1980; Mills and Morris, 1986; Bateson, 1983) and show the influence of mainstream "information literature".

platforms, consumers gather to talk about brands, products and services, in both positive terms – *co-advertising*, and negative terms – *co-destruction*. As stated by Plè and Caceres (2010) "inappropriate or unexpected use of the available resources in an interaction will result in value co-destruction for at least one of the parties". Consumer word of mouth and electronic word of mouth can be most usefully investigated by psychological theory.

In 2003, Bendalupi and Leone highlighted the psychological implication of interactivity. More recently, Gilde et al. (2011) described *customer citizenship behaviour*, or the discretionary response of a customer to external events, which require them to carry out functions other than consumption. If customers act as citizens, every opportunity offered by companies on social topics – pollution-free production, safety in the workplace, training, valorisation of immigration, equal opportunities, etc. – represents a new opportunity for dialogue and convergence. It is important to note that conversation about these topics can lead to effective results when the company is aware of being under observation by the crowd, even non-contractual observation.

Ate and Buttgen (2008) introduce as a sentiment the concept of *customer orientation to the company*, which can influence the mood of conversation between customer and company. In fact, customers' contributions are, in this light, a form of *organizational citizenship behaviour*, which clearly can be affected by cultural atmosphere (Bettencourt, 1997; Kendrick, 1985; Goudarzi, 2009). From this perspective, working customers can be seen as employees and the *socialization of their work* implies a strong commitment to the company (Bowers et al., 1990; Leary-Kelly et al., 1994; Manolis et al., 2001; Vijande et al., 2009).

What is clear is that the new social space belonging to the digital conversation is a new middle ground for matching or tuning between market and society. In the new digital space, individuals talk as customers and citizens at the same time. Cova and Dalli (2007, 2009) suggest that the new collective conversations can be epitomized by the concept of communities. Within communities, individuals are inspired by linking value or *gift logic* and aim to defend society. The authors ask whether this type of meta-market can be considered as an entity in itself, separate from the market and capable of protecting citizens from the risk of exploitation. From the same perspective, other authors focus on the concept of "sharing", as a fundamental consumer behaviour that is similar to gift giving (Bergquist and Ljiungberg, 2001; Belk, 2010).

Starting from the idea of newly-shared collective conversation, a new type of convergence is coming into being. Market and society do not coincide; companies and customers act as counterparts playing different roles, but their interests are converging. New concepts like *reciprocity* and *social trust* have entered the marketing dictionary (Mathwick, Wiertz, and de Ruyter, 2008; Uzoamak and Jeffrey, 1999; Paulin, Ferguson and Bergeron, 2006; Feldman, 1981; Buttgen, 2008; Fisher, 1986; Jeong and Lee, 2013).

In some cases, prosumerism can generate a new loop between corporate and consumer responsibility, and consumers can commit to the new social game of being a customer and citizen at work. Nevertheless, the risk of exploitation is just around the corner.

4.   Convergence

As we have seen, the working customers' revolution can be interpreted from two conflicting points of view. Optimists describe a sort of web democracy with the benefits of a new collective intelligence able to inform new business models and create new value. They believe that many industries, such as music, media, information technology, finance, retailing, gaming, entertainment and tourism are being positively revolutionized by customers' work. Pessimists warn that it is precisely in the sectors where this revolution is taking place that customers are most at risk of exploitation. We shall now develop a new perspective called *convergence*: market and society do not coincide, companies and customers act as counterparts and have different roles, but their interests can converge in the new social space belonging to the sharing economy and to peer-to-peer communities.

Public Scrutiny

This third perspective is taken by researchers who study the collective counter-power of peer-to-peer conversations. According to this literature, market and society do not coincide but may converge towards common interests in the new social space belonging the peer-to-peer communities. This means that the company accepts a new mechanism of collective indirect control or "Public Scrutiny" (Kozinets, 2002), or people's ethical control of the topic online. In practice, individuals take part in peer-to-peer conversation with a mixture of narcissism and altruism in order to feel they belong to a community, gain recognition and continue their process of identity building. Since identity is built on differences, in many cases the new collective conversations are driven by a reaction against market power (Dholakia, Cabusas and Wilcox, 2009).

But, can citizens exploit companies in the new social game?

The reciprocity of risks

Empirical studies of the working customer demonstrate that customer behaviour is often opportunistic and can hinder the control of co-service production (Kelley, Donnelly and Skinner, 1990; Zeithaml and Bitner, 2003; Vijande, Mieres and Sanches, 2009), as well as reduce company productivity (Chase, 1978, 1981; Goodwin, 1988; Gudergan, Wilden and Lings, 2009). These studies demonstrate that active consumer participation in the supply of a physical service does not always lead to economic benefits for the firm. Examples are the non-replacement of trays in self-service eateries and the number of thefts occurring in self-service shops selling goods with high unit value (Pellegrini, Minani and Munehiko, 2010).

Optional customer contributions are in this light a form of "organizational citizenship behaviour" (Bettencourt, 1997; Kendrick, 1985; Goudarzi, 2009). The issue of reciprocity of risks and benefits appears more complex when prosumerism becomes digital and thus has the potential to revolutionize a business model[9].

We now focus on what occurs when the new forms of dialogue are promoted by companies or spontaneously implemented by consumers freely sharing their knowledge. From a perspective of convergence it is important to establish whether companies and citizens are effectively finding

---

[9] Although there is a great deal of literature on the economic effects of prosumerism on the supply side, the issue of reciprocity between suppliers and customers is not much considered. To pinpoint the concept of reciprocity we can cite an example of physical prosumerism: the recent introduction of new self-scanning systems in supermarkets. Here the consumer is required to work by adding up the bill and thus giving the retailer the chance to save money on labour at the cash desk. In exchange, the retailer invests in appropriate technology without raising prices, thus giving the consumer a new service. Efforts and gifts are made by both parties, it is clearly not a case of giving something for nothing. It could be argued that the firm in making less effort, and in fact gains, but at the same time the functional benefits – no queues at the cashdesk and checks on amount spent – are greatly appreciated by customers. The same is true of new self-service systems offered by banks to reduce labour costs and test new forms of assistance.

new common ground for conversation or if, on the contrary, companies are simply exploiting the new fashion of social responsibility.

According to many authors, voluntarism, reciprocity, and social trust play important roles within communities. Recently, Gilde et al. (2011) described "customer citizenship behaviour", or the discretionary activity by a customer in response to external events which require him or her to carry out functions other than consumption. Every opening by companies on social topics is an opportunity for new forms of cooperation with citizens: pollution-free production, safety in the workplace, training, valorisation of immigration, equal opportunities, etc.

It is important to note is that conversation can lead to effective results when it depends directly on the interactions between citizens and companies. This can occur for environmental issues and for conversation directed to the public within the company. In fact, the "socialization of employees work" implies strong commitment as employees are first of all citizens (Vijande, Mieres and Sanches, 2009; Uzoamaka and Jeffrey, 1999; Paulin, Ferguson and Bergeron, 2006; Feldman, 1981; Buttgen, 2008; Fisher, 1986). From this perspective, co-working citizens can be seen as employees while at the same time employees can be seen as customers (Bowers, Martin and Luker, 1990; Leary-Kelly et al., 1994). A company which understands this fact and is open to dialogue with citizens cannot but invest in its own workers at the same time. In the best case, this implies a convergence between external and internal communication (Salmon, 2008; Mosseberg et al., 2006). Ate and Buttgen (2008), rather than "company orientation to the customers" describe "customer orientation to the company" that is a sentiment which can be affected by cultural atmosphere[10]. These issues are important; they could in fact lead to the de-construction or destruction of online communities" potential (Plé and Lefebvre, 2009; Uzoamaka and Jeffrey, 1999).

Finally, it appears that the new social game is very dangerous for companies that decide to take part in the dialogue without being more ethical.

---

[10] In the Italian market, for example, a strong trade union tradition and an undeveloped managerial culture have created deep division between capital and labour and between blue and white collar workers. According to Edelman Research, in Italy consumer trust of companies is the lowest in Europe: only 27% of Italian consumers consider companies trustworthy compared to the European average of 42%.

The new forms of collective interaction indeed appear to be leading to new informal rules, which favour trust and act as barriers against exploitation. This implies that there is a shift taking place from external sanction mechanisms towards new, self-regulated processes which reward honest behaviour. In this perspective, any conversation on society is welcome because even if it is market-driven, it may still have an important effect. Consumers can themselves be involved in the process, encouraged by companies to take part in new sustainability awareness schemes. Companies know that being under observation by the crowd means accepting a new mechanism of indirect control.

In the next chapter, we establish whether prosumerism can generate a new loop between companies and consumers' social responsibility, and whether consumers can commit to the new social game.

4.   Customers or citizens

The co-value model: a qualitative analysis

The recent attempt by companies to promote, intermediate and intercept the customer conversation are opening up a new ideological debate: is the new social game bringing new value for the gamers? Are we seeing a truly new form of value co-creation?

In this chapter we try to determine whether the new social game is actually providing wealth for players, and measure the growing overlap between dialogue and sale, between market and society, or more simply, between money and gift.

1.   The Co-value Model

As described in the introduction, we identify seven types of collaborations:

- Co-planning
- Co-production
- Co-advertising
- Co-selling
- Co-logistics
- Co-use
- Co-post use

and three combinations of players:

- One-to-many
- Many-to-many
- Peer-to-peer

In this framework, the metrics of the co-value model proposed by Pellegrini and De Canio (2016) suggest that individuals receive two types of value inputs:

1. *economic benefits* represented by their cognitive and affective perception of *functional* advantages such as price, quality and time saving;
2. *social benefits* classified as *personal* – me/identity, *relational* – us/ friends, and *social* – us/society.

The arrows going in different directions are the key feature of the diagram and indicate that these benefits are the result of more than one type of investment. For example, social benefits can accrue in all three phases of dialogue: pre-sale, sale and post-sale (Figure 1).

Figure 1   The co-value model

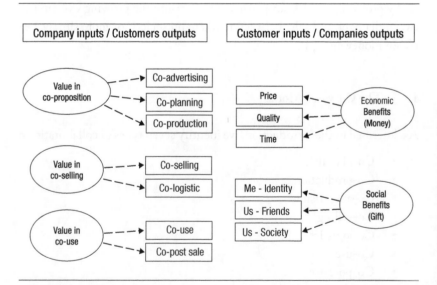

This logical framework should thus reveal how individuals react to external economic stimuli, driven by the logic of money, and to social stimuli, driven by the logic of gift; in other words we try to understand when and why individuals act as customers and/or citizen.

The model is applied to 20 crowdsourcing platforms including many of the ones proposed in the previous chapter, providing a topical focus on implications for management. The second component included in our model is more sociological and behavioural and focuses on response to external stimuli rather than individual psychology. An example is Muniz et al. (2009) who observe the best community practices able to enhance collaborative value creation. Methodologically, this is an interdisciplinary study, as it uses information from a naturalistic observation of community activities together with 'netnographic' analysis of consumer posts online. Among the many researchers in favour of an interdisciplinary approach, we find Addis and Podestà (2003) who discuss the methodological challenges posed by post-modernism, Cova (1997) who suggests the interdisciplinary use of different tools, and Kozinets (2010) who discusses the methodological anarchy current in the field. Following the experience of this recent research, our approach is inductive and does not include the use of questionnaires. The study focuses on cognitive, affective and behavioural reaction to stimuli from digital conversations. There are no interviews of consumers; their dialogue experience or electronic word-of-mouth (e-WOM) from 20 international crowdsourcing platforms is monitored instead.

2.   The factors influencing digital behaviour

According to consumer research literature, two sets of factors lead to the emergence of digital behaviour. The first set of factors are at the individual level, that is, within the person. These factors include personality traits, perception, experience and values (Lewin, 1951; Minsky and Marin, 1999; Davis, Bagozzi and Warshaw, 1989; Carlson and Zmud, 1999; Pagani, Hofacker and Goldsmith, 2011). The second set is external to the person, and consists of the environment surrounding the individual (Bendapudi and Leone., 2003; Maglio and Spohrer, 2008; Prahalad and Ramaswamy, 2004; Siano, Vollero and Palazzo, 2011; Suwelack, Hogreve and Hoyer, 2011). Our focus will be not on the psychological traits of digital co-workers – the first set – but on the psychological consequences of the new forms of dialogue – the second set. We again start from the analysis of company outputs to consumers – *consumers inputs* – and consumer outputs to companies – *company inputs*.

In each one of these phases, individuals have the opportunity to co-operate. Their reactions to these opportunities are filtered by a personal mind-set of cognitive, affective and behavioural traits.

Many authors point out that customer reactions are stimulated by information processing – cognitive vision – but that information processing requires physical support – experiential vision (Hirschman and Hoolbrook, 1982; Hirschman, 1986; Frijida, 1999; Kahneman, 2005). Thus, it is precisely new technologies and their vicarious capacity to reproduce experiences and transfer information which, in recombining the three phases of dialogue, sale and use, are today giving rise to new architectures of knowledge. In this context, physical experience remains at the core of many of the new business models. Lusch and Vargo (2004) write "Value is always uniquely and phenomenologically determined by the beneficiary..."[1].

In one of the first studies of prosumerism, Chase (1978) distinguishes forms of cooperation according to the extent of "physical presence of [the] customer in the system". Mills and Morris (1986), Faranda (1994) and later Payne, Storbacka and Frow (2008) base their classification system on the extent of interaction in order to identify the participation-intensive services. Wikstrom (1996) and Wilkstrom, Hedbon and Thuresson (2010) observe that interaction between consumers and companies involves design, production and marketing, as well as consumption and later destruction of products. Buttgen (2008) tests a model implying different phases of co-production, and Michel, Brown and Gallan (2008) identify different roles for the working consumer and different techniques used by suppliers to encourage consumer involvement. According to our first classification of the cooperation phases, customers can be involved before, during and after sale (Figure 1).

This point of view is being enriched by contributions from "experiential marketing" literature (Pine and Gilmore, 1999; Lusch and Vargo, 2008; Sundbo, 2009; Ravald, 2009; Felix and Sempels, 2009) but also by very recent research on experiential and social functioning of the brain (Weber,

---

[1] Lusch and Vargo use the adverb "phenomenologically" so that the experiential attribute does not call to mind staging or the Disneyland effect. The note appears to be an attempt to distance their work from the approach of Pine and Gilmore (1999). Sundbo (2009) writes, "The experience economy has recently received increasing attention, particularly in Northern Europe, as an economic growth area that attracts increased awareness. In some countries, such as Denmark and Sweden, the attention that it attracts is disproportionally large compared to its economic importance. This is probably caused by the aura of stars and celebrities that the field includes".

2007; Dalli, 2004, Kahneman, 2005; Freedberg and Gallese 2008, Zeki, 2007). It is probably not by chance that even today IKEA is the most frequently cited case of the working customer (Edvardsson and Enquist, 2002; Bitner et al., 1997; Kelley, Donnelly and Skinner, 1990; Dong, Evans and Shaoming, 2008)[2]. This call back to real, physical life perhaps lessens the risks of addiction noted above. And in any case it is significant that one of the key issues in the on-going revolution is the continuity between digital and physical conversation (Mandelli and Accoto, 2012).

Many empirical experiments suggest that the black box of customer choice is experience driven but always filtered by cognitive processes. Recently, Ravald (2009) has observed that "the customer response can be functionally or emotionally grounded... a good or a service does not have value from the customer viewpoint until a personal meaning has been ascribed to it". "Personal meaning" is not derived simply from utilisation or consumption; it requires cognitive processing. This is exemplified by the concept of "use and ownership": in the car industry, for example, ownership of the good has a symbolic and cognitive meaning and this restricts the growth of car-sharing, which offers car use but not car ownership (Felix and Sempels, 2009). So the value dimension of goods is mediated by rationality and culture, in other words by variables which are the outcome of long-term cognitive experience rather than short-term experiences or events.

In this context, Novak, Hoffman and Yung (2000) concentrate their focus on the *flow state*, which is a cognitive state experienced during online navigation. Preece (2001) identifies factors that affect online community usability and sociability. More recent methodological studies include Aaron and Mathew (2012), Villads Troye and Supphellen (2012), Shu and Peck (2011) and Pranić and Roehl (2012). Theoretical studies of this type are often enriched by laboratory tests on actual consumer behaviour when faced with goods and services. Fuchs, Prandelli and Schreier (2010), for example, test response of consumers to a T-shirt once they had been involved in its production. The work of Premazzi et

---

[2] Retail is a service sector that to a large extent has become experience-dominated, e.g. IKEA (Edvardsson and Enquist, 2008). Other authors studying retail from this perspective include Bitner et al. (1997), Kelley et al. (1990), Lugli (2005), Martinelli (2009), Kinney and Grewal (2008), Dong, Evans and Shaoming (2009), Montagnini and Sebastiani (2009) and Pellegrini (2001).

al. (2010) is also very interesting; a panel of consumers is offered similar rewards by different brands in an experiment to measure the role of trust. Pagani, Hofacker and Goldsmith (2010) adopt a psychological perspective and describe how personality traits of working customers influence their active and passive roles within communities. Here too behaviour is analysed by questionnaires administered to different clusters of consumers in order to build new measurement scales of contributive behaviour. These studies often measure cognitive, affective, sensorial and behavioural variables in order to describe the concept of experience (Zarantonello, 2008).

3.   Methodology: The qualitative analysis

In order to test our co-value model we divide the individual benefits into two categories: economic benefit and social benefit. Both inputs and outputs are measured through semantic mining of the key words used in online conversations. We aim to identify web sentiment through netnography analysis based on a sample of 20 crowdsourcing platforms, including, for example, Innocentive, Quora, TripAdvisor and Amazon Turk.

Netnography analysis as defined by Kozinets "provides information on the symbolism, meaning, and consumption patterns of online consumer groups… it is an online marketing research technique for providing consumer insight". We thus opt to use pure observational online ethnography to measure the normal flow of information that users exchange, without any kind of intermediation from sources as used in consumer behaviour analysis.

Conversation among participants from three sources: Facebook, Twitter and Google Blog, is monitored (see Appendix). The web voice was first monitored in May-June 2012, and in a second phase in May-June 2013. We gathered a total of 600 texts from each of 20 platforms investigated, reaching a database based in total on 12,600 texts. From these 12,600 texts we excluded:

- impersonal descriptions which give no information about the user's experience;
- all messages from bloggers who belong to the company;
- all messages which were too brief to decipher objectively.

This left us with 4,601 texts and a total of over 250,000 words in about 2,000 pages of word scripts describing the sentiment of consumers. We initially tested open software like T-Lab for preliminary linguistic screening, but the absence of a calibrated search engine for web monitoring of very different case histories showed the limits of automatism[3]. Therefore, we opted for a manual check of contents. Researchers were divided into 4 groups and a cross-linked system of checking words and phrases was used, so that if observers in one group were not unanimous in interpreting a message it was submitted to a group of specialists.

For each of the 4,601 texts, a deep semantic analysis was conducted[4]. The following examples briefly illustrate the workings of text mining. A simplified matrix of consumer inputs to the firm and related outputs is helpful to show the result of this first conceptual screening. Figures 2 and 3 below then show the conceptual framework of our model at work.

Figure 2   Text analyses from TripAdvisor website

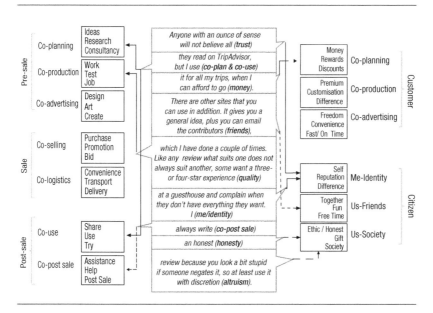

---

[3] See appendix for methodological details.
[4] See appendix for methodological details.

Figure 3 Text analyses from Pirate Bay website

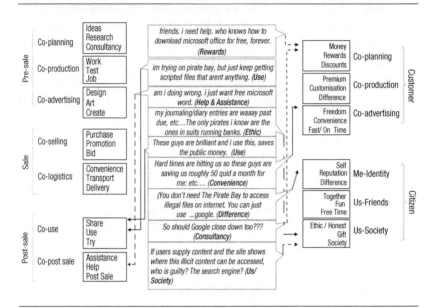

The Trip Advisor's and Pirate Bay's examples show how consumers' posts were decoded. The frequency of occurrence of the concepts is expressed as relative to a total of 100, but the original data-set contains multiple frequencies.

4. Hypotheses

In order to verify the robustness of the proposed model, we focus on three research hypotheses:

• *Hypotesis 1: Contemporarity: conversations enable the actors (companies and individuals) to exchange multiple inputs and outputs before, during and after the sale. This means that the traditional divide between value creation – R&D, production and advertising – and value distribution and consumption – sale, use and post use – is blurring.*

Several case histories show actors co-acting at the same time in more than one process (Table 1). The overview shows that co-advertising is the pro-

Table 1　Findings of web monitoring of 4,601 texts – Relative frequency of concepts

	Co-planning & research	Co-production	Co-advertising & communication	Co-selling	Co-logistics	Co-use	Co-post use	Price	Quality	Time	Me - Identity	Friends - Us	Society - Gift - Us	Number of texts
CO-PLANNING (collective research & innovation)														
INNOCENTIVE – co-research & prize contest	41.0	27.5	23.2	1.1	4.8	2.4	–	24.0	3.5	1.7	5.9	13.9	51.0	408
CITY 2.0 – knowledge sharing	88.2	–	11.8	–	–	–	–	5.7	1.4	–	11.6	3.0	78.3	136
CO-PRODUCTION (collective contents & tasks)														
HUFFINGTON POST – user generated contents	10.0	51.2	28.7	–	3.7	6.2	–	3.3	53.3	2.2	13.3	10.6	17.2	166
AMAZON TURK – cloud labor/microtasks	–	100.0	–	–	–	–	–	43.7	15.1	21.1			20.1	57
QUORA – research tasks	10.0	40.0	30.0	–	–	20.0	–		53.1	14.3	14.3	4.1	14.3	92
CO-COMMUNICATION (collective creativity)														
KLOUT – social rating	–	–	50.0	25.0	–	25.0	–	2.1	23.7	9.9	28.1	13.5	22.7	176
THREADLESS – product customization	21.0	–	75.0	2.2	–	1.8	–	13.1	3.0	11.3	21.8	18.8	32.2	271
MOUNTAIN DEW – product selection	18.6	20.7	39.5	4.2	16.9	–	–	4.8	37.1	2.1	14.6	6.0	35.4	342
CO-SELLING (collective or interactive shopping)														
EBAY – e-commerce	4.3	–	10.2	53.6	21.7	1.4	8.7	34.2	38.4	9.5	6.5	0.8	10.6	300
FAB – content markets	–	–	66.0	20.0	–	–	14.0	9.6	34.0	9.6	27.9	11.2	7.6	200
GROUPON – buying groups	6.7	–	–	40.0	13.3	20.0	20.0	31.4	41.4	3.1	7.9	15.2	1.0	162
CO-LOGISTIC (collective or interactive logistic)														
FACEBOOK PLACES – check-in	–	–	32.0	23.0	35.0	10.0	–	6.1	39.8	–	3.3	11.0	39.8	209
DOMINOS – delivery	9.0	–	–	–	42.0	19.0	30.0	8.3	56.0	15.6	6.9	7.3	6.0	300
NEXTDOOR – physical sharing	10.8	8.1	8.1	8.1	13.5	45.0	6.3	4.3	38.0	2.2	–	13.0	42.4	181
CO-USE (collective & peer-to-peer cooperation)														
WARCRAFT – game sharing	14.5	–	52.7	23.6	–	9.1	–	16.0	16.0	25.7	20.2	10.2	11.8	407
DROPBOX – joint application	7.0	–	47.3	2.8	–	40.0	2.8	20.1	64.4	0.8	5.3	6.1	3.4	200
AIRBNB – house sharing	19.6	2.2	19.6	38.7	–	20.0	–	37.3	27.0	5.0	2.1	20.3	8.3	266
CO-POST USE (collective & peer-to-peer cooperation)														
TRIPADVISOR – service rating	39.1	–	4.4	–	4.4	–	52.2	8.1	64.7	0.6	4.0	4.6	17.9	220
PINTEREST – social commerce	27.2	–	24.5	11.7	–	6.4	30.1	4.0	12.0	17.3	32.0	9.3	25.3	409
PIRATE WAY – downloading	–	–	40.0	–	–	30.0	30.0	16.3	38.4	1.2	8.1	5.8	30.2	99
Total/Average	18.0	8.3	29.7	14.1	8.8	11.1	10.0	14.4	30.5	8.4	12.9	9.9	23.7	4,601

cess with the highest level of consumer involvement (29.7%) followed by co-planning of goods and services (18%), co-selling (14.1%), use (11.1%), co-post-sales (10.0%), co-logistics (8.8%) and co-production (8.3%).

• *Hypotesis 2: Collective responsibility: conversations are often focussed on collective or plural topics – us/friends–us/society. This requires the company to accept a new mechanism of social or collective control.*

In order to test this hypothesis, we ranked the conversations on the basis of three variables: identity–me, relationship-friends and society-us.

The first five communities involving a strong element of me-identity, often appear well-positioned in terms of relationship-friends and society-us. There are also intermediate situations like Groupon where consumers show interest in sharing purchase coupons with friends but do not find the game innovative enough to provide a distinction of self-identity. Overall, there are few communities where the consumer gives a low value to friendship (Amazon MTurk, eBay, City 2.0). Moreover, values are very high in the "society" variables and reveal an increasing awareness of the ethical implications of being continuously connected (Figure 4).

Figure 4   The percentage of Identity: me – identity; friends – us; society – gift

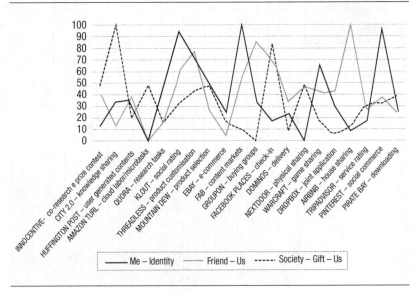

• *Hypotesis 3: Convergence: Actors' conversations are focussed not only on customers' benefits – price quality and time – but also on citizens' benefits – identity, friends, and society. This leads to a new equilibrium or convergence between the customer perspective – logic of money – and the citizen perspective – logic of gift.*

The fact that the social variables were cited in almost all the texts shows that the risk of consumer exploitation exists, but that it is largely balanced out by consumer attention to the social content of services. What is significant is that consumer and citizen interests do not appear in inverted order. For example, it could be objected that communities like eBay and Groupon have a very small social dimension, but as a matter of fact, we found that dialogue is often about following the rules, and about the experiential and psychological dimension of use (Figure 5). These are frequent signals that the convergence of interests are not taken for granted, and many consumers comment on the need to be careful about their rewards. It is precisely this explicit mention of risks that comprises of a defence mechanism against negative aspects of the convergence taking place. From our point of view, this is new evidence of the convergence between the customer perspective – *logic of money* – and the citizen perspective – *logic of gift*.

Figure 5   Ranking of communities based on the concept of money and gift

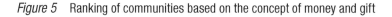

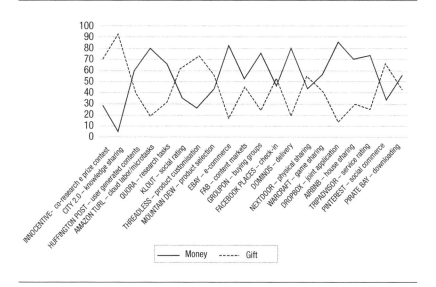

5.   Overview

With the aim of analysing in dept the Convergence hypotesis we compared the intensity of relationships between inputs and outputs of the
co-value model and we tested a bivariate correlation with two different
levels of significance, 0.01 and 0.05. Our sample shows the first set of
relations (Table 2).

Table 2 Internal relationships between different types of content of conversations

		Price	Quality	Time	Me - Identity	Friend - Us	Society - Gift - Us
Co-planning	Pearson Correlation	0.069	-0.240	0.122	0.264	0.279	0.675**
	Sig. (2-Tailed)	0.774	0.308	0.610	0.260	0.234	0.001
	N	20	20	20	20	20	20
Co-production	Pearson Correlation	-0.079	-0.268	-0.265	-0.204	-0.111	0.312
	Sig. (2-Tailed)	0.741	0.253	0.258	0.388	0.642	0.181
	N	20	20	20	20	20	20
Co-advertising & communication	Pearson Correlation	0.062	-0.167	0.498*	0.695**	0.539*	0.332
	Sig. (2-Tailed)	0.827	0.481	0.026	0.001	0.014	0.153
	N	20	20	20	20	20	20
Co-selling	Pearson Correlation	0.718**	0.131	0.427	0.232	0.304	-0.118
	Sig. (2-Tailed)	-	0.583	0.061	0.325	0.193	0.621
	N	20	20	20	20	20	20
Co-logistics	Pearson Correlation	0.069	0,506*	0.006	-0.169	-0.053	0.153
	Sig. (2-Tailed)	0.773	0.023	0.805	0.477	0.826	0.521
	N	20	20	20	20	20	20
Co-use	Pearson Correlation	0.121	0.316	0.085	-0.112	0.266	-0.304
	Sig. (2-Tailed)	0.610	0.175	0.720	0.629	0.257	0.193
	N	20	20	20	20	20	20
Co-post sale	Pearson Correlation	-0.124	0.379	0.265	0.329	-0.043	-0.056
	Sig. (2-Tailed)	0.603	0.099	0.259	0.157	0.856	0.814
	N	20	20	20	20	20	20

Note: ** Correlation is significant at the 0,01 level (2-tailed)
          * Correlation is significant at the 0,05 level (2-tailed)

Firstly we observe that co-advertising is the co-creation construct with the highest level of consumer involvement since individuals' conversations are strongly influenced by the social desire to share personal experiences, knowledge and opinions about the companies or brands with which they interact.

As seen in Table 2, co-advertising proves to be closely correlated to me-identity with a Pearson correlation of r^2: 0.695 at 0.01 significance. This relationship is explained by the individual wishing to "be original" and the emotive involvement of individuals using their own creativity. Moreover, co-advertising appears closely correlated to friend-us with a Pearson correlation of r^2: 0.539 at 0.05 significance. Lastly, co-advertising proves to be closely correlated to time, with a Pearson correlation of r^2: 0.498 at 0.05 significance. This last functional benefit can be explained by the "time saving" benefit for individuals who are collecting information about the products which they are going to purchase. Those correlations are graphically presented in our model, shown in Figure 6.

As seen in Table 2, a new and very significant correlation appears between co-selling and price, with a Pearson correlation of ρ:0.718 at 0.01 significance. This relationship can be explained by the fact that customers who are involved in co-selling focus their conversations on Financial benefit of the exchange.

Figure 6 The effects of co-advertising on the co-value model

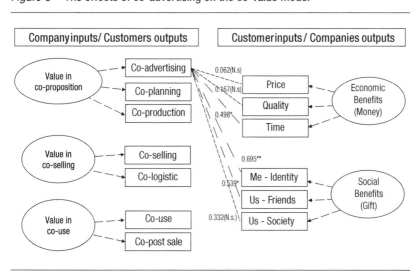

A second univocal correlation is between co-logistics and quality, with a Pearson correlation of ρ:0.506 at 0.05 significance. This relationship is explained by the functional goals of this form of cooperation, which mean customers discuss new forms of cooperation enabled by physical or logistical conditions.

A third group of significant and multiple relationships is connected to co-planning activities. First of all, we observe that co-planning is closely correlated to society/gift/us, with a Pearson correlation of ρ:0.675 at 0.01 significance. From a theoretical point of view, these relationships introduce a rational and cognitive interpretation of social sensitivity. People commenting on their personal experience of co-planning use words, phrases and sentences which show their awareness of being socially responsible.

Last, but not least, it is necessary to observe the weak correlations between co-use and co-post use and social benefits. This is partially surprising because friendship and society were expected to be at the core of co-use and co-post use activities.

Starting from this last finding, we analized in depth the semantic difference between friendship – *us, friends, together, fun, enjoyment…* – and society – *ethic, honest, responsible… –.*

With this goal we tested Principal Component Analysis (PCA) so as to reduce the amount of redundant information. We then found two new latent variables (Components 1 and 2) into the model (Table 3). These two components in fact explain 68.88% of the original variance of outputs.

Component 1 comprises of the emotive world of "creativity, individual and friends" and Component 2 comprises the rational world of "planning, price, quality and society". The positioning of the 20 communities can be almost fully described by the two new components (Figure 5).

The 20 platforms studied clearly have different vocations. It is possible to identify a strong vocation for the emotive world of "creativity, individual and friends" for platforms such as Warcraft or Pinterest, or for others like City 2.0, Nextdoor or TripAdvisor, more focused on the rational world of "planning, price, quality and society".

A platform like Innocentive proves to be ranked quite high in both these factors. More generally each community shows a mix of the two components but the co-use and co-post use platforms, like Warcraft, Dropbox, Tripadvisor, Pinterest, Pirate Bay or Airbnb, in which we'll focus on the next chapter, don't get higher scores than average. Their ethical performance was expected to be higher since their functioning is often

Table 3   Component analysis

Components	Initial Eigenvalues			Extraction sum of squarted loadings		
	Total	% of variance	Cumulative %	Total	% of variance	Cumulative %
1	4,272	47,470	47,470	4,272	47,470	47,470
2	1,927	21,413	68,882	1,927	21,413	68,882
3	,863	9,585	78,467			
4	,626	6,951	85,417			
5	,466	5,173	90,591			
6	,321	3,566	94,156			
7	,213	2,368	96,525			
8	,208	2,306	98,831			
9	,105	1,169	100,00			

Figure 5   Crowdsourcing platform positioning

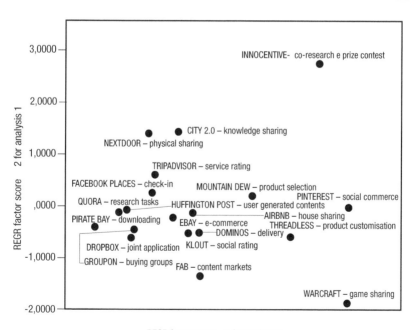

based on peer-to-peer models whit individuals called to be producers and users at the same time. Starting from this evidence in the next chapter we'll focus on two peer-to-peer digital platforms: BlaBlaCar and Airbnb. In these cases, citizens will be called to share not only conversation but also money.

Consequently, ther efforts will put into question borders between economic and social benefits of the collaboration.

5.   The collaborative consumption

BlaBlaCar vs. Airbnb: a quantitative analysis

Starting from the previous results we focus now on two peer-to-peer digital platform: BlaBlaCar and Airbnb. In these cases individuals are called to share not only words but also money and this effort puts into question borders between economic and social benefits of the collaborative consumption.

1.   The collaborative consumption

In collaborative consumption, the provider and the user of the service are both consumers. Collaborative consumption represents "the peer-to-peer based activity of obtaining, giving, or sharing the access to goods and services, coordinated through community-based online services" (Hamari, Sjöklint and Ukkonen, 2016, p. 1). As is clear from this definition, collaborative consumption is mainly focused on the creation of value from consumers to other consumers. In the literature, collaborative consumption is defined as a hybrid business model that involves both the owning and gifting of products and services while transactions are supported by community online services (Hamari, Sjöklint and Ukkonen, 2016). In this vein Rachel Botsman, a leading researcher on collaborative consumption, states on her website that "the reinvention of traditional market behaviours – renting, lending, swapping, sharing, bartering, gifting – through technology, is taking place in ways and on a scale not possible before the Internet". In the same way, Belk identifies temporary access to non-ownership models of utilizing consumer goods and services and the web as the main two communities between sharing and collaborative consumption. Hamari, Sjöklint and Ukkonen (2016) find that people involved in collaborative consumption are motivated by sustainability factors, enjoyment and economic gains. Collaborative consumption is a good example of the sharing economy in which people are motivated by the two aspects of money and gift, in terms of economic benefits and sustainable consumption, as well as by the new social aspect of enjoyment provided by the activity itself (John, 2013). It is based on the ancestral impulse or the "natural behavioural instinct of sharing and exchanging" (Botsman and Rogers, 2011, p. 213). So collaborative consumption can be described as a sharing economy phenomenon of production and consumption (John, 2013).

Collaborative consumption has enabled new forms of value creation, and in many cases, new business models have created hitherto non-existent markets (Mahadevan, 2000). On one hand, consumers are able to communicate via online platforms, evaluating and comparing products and services, which creates both economic and social benefits (Pellegrini and De Canio, 2016). On the other hand, consumers themselves are becoming providers of products and services by means of sharing platforms (Price and Belk, 2016). Consequently, the web has supported the creation of start-up companies able to fill gaps in supply.

In some cases, these new business models are perceived by users as indistinguishable from traditional services (Price and Belk, 2016; Möhlmann, 2015).

In agreement with Price and Belk (2016) who write, "it is difficult to precisely define and distinguish from market and gift-giving exchanges" (p. 193), we can support the idea that new hybrid business models are developing thanks to new forms of market supply which place the individual at the centre of both supply and consumption.

As we shall see in the description of some of the more successful collaborative consumption platforms, they have in fact digitalized a supply gap; and over time, strong market demand has enabled the development of more than one platform for each need. The level of competition between platforms offering the same product and/or service is very high. Nevertheless, at the moment, the market appears to be big enough for all of them; those who are really suffering from the spread of digital platforms for collaborative consumption are operators on the traditional market.

In the following pages we present two of case studies that have revolutionized the sector of hospitality and travel in Italy and worldwide.

2.   Car sharing: The BlaBlaCar case

Car sharing has become more widespread in the last 20 years as a popular alternative to car ownership (Bardhi and Eckhardt, 2012).

As noted in chapter 1 we can observe at least three models of car sharing.

The first one is the case of a one-to-many car sharing service. It consists in a group of paying individuals who access a fleet of cars along with other paying members periodically over time. Cars are used almost exclusively for short, local trips, as the cost becomes prohibitive for longer distances. In this case, the service is provided by a third player, public or private, who rents out a car to someone requiring transport for a short period of time. As the car sharing is provided by a company it is not an example of collaborative consumption. One of the most famous car sharing services in Italy is Enjoy, developed by Eni Smart Consumer S.p.A. It is available in 5 Italian cities: Florence, Milan, Rome, Turin and Catania. A total of 1,084 red vehicles, both cars (Fiat 500) and scooters (Piaggio MP3), can be booked by people for a limited period of time. Using a mobile app, people find the nearest vehicle and rent it for the time they need. The cost is calculated on the number of minutes the vehicle is used. In this way, the same vehicle can be used and shared between individuals. Car sharing is not a typical example of collaborative consumption, as the service is offered by a company.

In this case the promoter is also the supplier of the service, so the model is clearly one-to-many (Enjoy to customers).

The second case is a many-to-many car sharing. It's the case of a private taxi service platform like Uber, the promoter is simple aggregating many private professional suppliers in a many-to-many framework (Uber to drivers and customers).

Uber – whose slogan is "Find the way: creating possibilities for riders, drivers and cities" – is the biggest on-demand taxi service worldwide. Individuals with a car offer a taxi-service to other individuals. Ubercab was founded in March 2009 by Travis Kalanick and Garrett Camp in San Francisco, California. In a few years Uber reached 58 countries and is today valued at $62.5 billion (techcrunch.com, July 2016). The idea of Uber was born "on a snowy Paris evening" in which the founders had trouble hailing a cab". The supply gap they noticed gave them the idea of creating an alternative to traditional taxi service. They created an app to request a taxi following the idea that people should be able to request "what they want, when they want it" by using technology. On one hand, drivers earn money using the app, and on the other hand users receive a quick and secure service, and cities strengthen their local economies, improve access to transportation and make streets safer (Uber website – our story).

All communication and transactions between drivers and passengers are made using the Uber app. The platform thus guarantees the identity of drivers and passengers, and at the same time reduces risks connected with payment, also reducing payment time. Uber takes 20% of each ride for its brokerage service between drivers and passengers, and the driver earns the remaining 80%. Uber is in competition with the strictly regulated taxi sector, and for this reason, is not currently available in many countries, including Italy.

Finally, we assist to a third model where the car is provided by users is spreading and is called carpooling. Carpooling is a different form of car sharing.

The term carpooling indicates a travel option in which travellers share the car with the aim of reducing travel costs. It is often used by commuters. Provided and used by individuals, carpooling is a typical example of collaborative consumption.

In a platform like BlaBlaCar the promoter aggregates not professional players but citizens in a peer-to-peer perspective (BlaBlaCar to citizens).

BlaBlaCar is the largest worldwide community that allows drivers and passengers to share their trips. The platform connects drivers with free seats and passengers wishing to travel in the same direction, allowing them to share the travel costs and time. The service is currently available on three continents and in 22 countries. The community counts 35 million users and is accessible both via the website and app.

What differences are there from the point of view of individuals? Are individuals aware of the difference between a car sharing service like Enjoy, a private taxi service platform like Uber and a peer-to-peer platform like BlaBlaCar? Before answering let's introduce a new case.

STORY TELLER – HOW BLABLACAR STARTED

The idea of BlaBlaCar was born one Christmas when I wanted to get home to my family in the French countryside. At 500km away from Paris, it wasn't the easiest place to reach. With no car and all the trains sold out, I finally convinced my younger sister to make a lengthy detour via Paris to pick me up. During the journey home, I noticed something. I could see the train from the A10 highway. The train that I should have been on. The train that was overbooked and had no seats left. And whizzing by me were hundreds of cars. Cars that were mostly empty, except for the driver. Suddenly I realized what I was actually seeing. There were seats available but they weren't on trains, they were in CARS!

For the next 72 hours, I couldn't sleep. In each empty car seat, I saw a gap in the market and was convinced that other people would benefit from such an affordable, convenient and friendly transport solution. Could empty seats in existing cars be the beginning of a new travel network?

I knew I didn't want to develop the idea alone so I kicked off the first version of BlaBlaCar with a good friend and former colleague. As I was constantly on the lookout for ways to further develop the idea, I started attending entrepreneurial meet-ups in Paris. That's where I met fellow co-founder Francis Nappez who had a strong experience in developing and building digital architecture for high-traffic websites. During that same period I also enrolled in the one-year MBA programme at INSEAD Business School. That's when I met fellow co-founder Nicolas Brusson who had strong venture capital experience from past roles in Silicon Valley and London.

It was after graduating from the MBA programme at the end of 2007 that I decided to jump full-time into the project. 2008 was perhaps one of the hardest years in my life but there were now 70,000 people using the platform and the business' massive potential was fostering an unstoppable motivation. I realized that Francis and Nicolas each brought complementary skills to the table and it felt absolutely right to share the direction of the company with them.

It took another five years for BlaBlaCar to reach its first million members and achieve the liquidity that sparked viral growth. Over time we tested several different strategies and business models and I feel there are four things which have been key to getting to where we are today: 1) Creating online interpersonal trust and thereby unlocking the potential of sharing at scale; 2) finding the right business model to make the activity sustainable; 3) thinking of a product by its usage and staying close to our members; and 4) creating a working environment that encourages innovation.

By the end of 2016, BlaBlaCar will count 40 million members in 22 countries. In the past decade, enabled by trust and technology, we've built the world's largest carpooling community. We have turned millions of lonely drivers into carpoolers and have opened up a whole new world of friendly and affordable travel. We are optimising cars, one of the world's most inefficiently used assets. And best of all, we are enabling new social connections along the way.

Frédéric Mazzella – Founder of BlaBlaCar

3.   Home-sharing: The Airbnb case

As noted by Heo (2016), one of the main sectors in which the sharing economy and the collaborative consumption are booming is tourism. Indeed, the rise of "profit-based online platforms [has] changed the way people travel and is of great significance to the traditional tourism industry" (Heo, 2016, p. 2). Giving hospitality to friends and relatives in the home is a time-honoured custom. In some cultures it is one of the pillars of society in that it generates value. Having someone stay over in fact consolidates relationships and highlights positive values, and is emotively important in the benefits for the individuals involved. Hospitality also has an economic aspect; it makes travel easier as the host is familiar with the area and can give advice. It encourages tourism and makes it less costly. So even where no money changes hands, hospitality generates both economic and social value.

For all these reasons, hospitality has generated new forms of business. For example, in 1999 US programmer Casey Fenton founded CouchSurfing International which aimed to put those seeking and those offering accommodations into contact. In 2004, a non-profit company was set up by member donations. The service – with the slogan "Stay with Locals and Meet Travellers" – is free and is based on the desire to meet and share experiences with local people and other travellers. There are also monthly meetings of couchsurfers in many big cities, which give more opportunities to meet people, make friends, and be part of a community and find out about the area directly. Couchsurfing has become so important that today it is the world's largest travel community, with 15 million members in over 230 nations worldwide. The website www.couchsurfing.com shows it has 400,000 hosts, and 4 million surfers; 100,000 events are held in 20,000 cities around the world every year. It changed from a non-profit organization to a commercial company in 2011, but has remained free of charge to use. A small monthly membership fee however gives higher visibility to your profile, access to certain parts of the website and the mobile app, text messaging services and assistance in choosing accommodations and guests – in other words a safer and more reliable service.

Another platform that allows individuals to offer accommodation to peers is Airbnb. In fact, in Airbnb people can rent their own accommodation from those that rent out their room or their entire properties on a website. At the moment, Airbnb is considered the largest room rental platform in the world. As reported by Anna Vital (2014) in the blog Funders and Founders, the idea of Airbnb was developed in 2007 by two young-sters unable to pay their rent. Joe Gebbia and Brian Chesky, based in San Francisco, had the idea of renting out three air-mattresses plus breakfast on the web. Thus, they create a website called "*airbedandbreakfast.com*" in which they posted their offer. Two men and a woman were willing to pay $80 each (Figure 1). In 2008 a new co-founder, Nathan Blecharczyk was included in the project and the website link was simplified to Airbnb.com. As they had no money to develop their business, Brian, Joe and Nathan began to sell cereal boxes and raised $30,000, which they used to expand their company (Pagliaro, 2015).

In 2008, Airbnb arrived in Italy, but the real growth has been seen in just recent years. "Over the past eight years, Italy residents have formed a vibrant Airbnb community, sharing unique experiences with travellers from around the world" (Airbnb, 2016, p. 1). By 2015, the Airbnb Italian community consisted of 83,300 hosts and 3.6 millions guests who spend on average 3.6 nights in each stay, compared to the 3.0 nights that travel-lers spend in traditional Italian accommodations. As reported by Airbnb, hosts earn on average €2,300 a year, renting their house or room for 26 days/year.

Nowadays, Italy represents the third largest Airbnb community world-wide after the US and France (Airbnb, 2015; Avireddy, Ramamirtham and Subramanian).

Airbnb is the largest peer-to-peer community for accommodation worldwide. It is present in 191 countries and 34,000 cities and is used by 60 million guests (Möhlmann, 2015). One of its key elements of success is the supervision of the quality of renters which is guaranteed by a robust referee system. The system invites both hosts and guests to comment on their experience at the end of their stay, and also asks all users to complete a personal profile accurately with pictures and self-description.

So what benefits are expected by individuals? Are they the same of BlaBlaCar?

For example, as reported on the Airbnb website, the reasons for using Airbnb vary between people and include the following:

- *Guests*: "This market segment involves mostly those who *enjoy traveling* and at the same time *not spending all of their money* in a hotel room. They would rather spend it *visiting tourist sites* while they travel because they will *not be spending much time* where they will be staying. Some travellers rather stay somewhere they can relax and spend most of their days without emptying their pockets" (Airbnb, 2015).

- *Hosts*: "These include owners or renters who are willing to rent out their places. The reasons vary as well. They might want to *make some money* out of an unoccupied space or simply they just want to *meet interesting people*. Whatever the reason is, all hosts are looking to list their current place on Airbnb because they have the ability to get to know who will be staying in their property" (Airbnb, 2015).

Guttentag (2013) defines Airbnb as a disruptive innovation. Helped by the Internet, it has been able to establish a "novel business model [...] which centres on cost-saving, household amenities, and the potential for a more authentic local experience" (p. 1192).

4.   The conceptual model

As previously seen, economic (money) and social (gift) benefits drive the active role of consumers in the value chain. Starting from the qualitative analysis of the previous chapter we will now look at the phenomenon in depth and measure it by means of a questionnaire submitted to real users of two collaborative consumption platforms: Airbnb and BlaBlaCar.

Focusing on peer-to-peer exchange of a hospitality service (home-sharing) and a car service we examine some details.

In the cases we are going to analyse, we ask whether the provider derives both a financial benefit equivalent to the value of the shared room or apartment, and a social value feeling of being an active producer of value for society. And we ask whether guests have a double financial benefit deriving from access to a service cheaper than the traditional hotel or transport services and a social advantage of feeling like an active part in maintaining value in society.

Starting from our initial co-value model, in which customer and companies collaborate in value creation (Figure 1, chapter 4), we identify a sub model in which (Figure 1) the roles of producer and of user are both played by consumers.

Figure 1   The Co-value Model in Collaborative Consumption

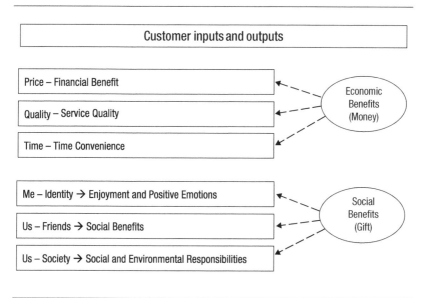

In the collaborative consumption model too, both economic and social benefits can be identified. On one hand, economic benefits compensate for the need to save money (Financial Benefit), receive a quality service (Service Quality) and reduce the access time to the service (Time Convenience).

On the other hand, social benefits have been identified in the pleasure of sharing products and services with other peers (Enjoyment and Positive Emotions), the opportunity to meet new people and share an experience with locals (Social Benefits) and generate a positive return for society both in terms of rewards (Social Responsibility) and environmental impact (Environmental Responsibility).

An online survey was administered to a panel of actual users of two large collaborative consumption platforms, Airbnb and BlaBlaCar. The questionnaire measured items on a 7-point Likert scale adapted from sharing-economy literature. It was distributed through a Qualtrics panel. The survey was conducted over a period of one week in October 2016.

5.   Determinants of peer-to-peer exchanges

It is clear that collaborative consumption can be considered a business model *sui generis* that generates economic value for society in the double form of transactions and savings (Bardhi and Eckhardt, 2012). Moreover, the possibility to share a part of one's own excess resources with society heightens the feeling of social belonging, and this produces welfare for society.

So the drivers of participation in collaborative consumption can be hypothesised to be as follows:

1) *Financial Benefits*

People involved in collaborative consumption are motivated by economic gains (Hamari, Sjöklint and Ukkonen, 2016; Möhlmann, 2015; Tussyadiah, 2015). Unlike sharing, where the economic exchange is not direct and immediate, but implicit and deferred, in collaborative consumption people are driven precisely by economic exchange and reciprocity (Bardhi and Eckhardt, 2012; Belk, 2010). Specifically in the context of collaborative consumption, economic benefits are generated both for service providers who share part of their surplus, earning money, and for users, who save money accessing cheaper offers. As stated by John (2013) the need to save money is higher in a context of economic difficulty; which is probably why we have seen an increase in collaborative consumption in recent years. We therefore postulate a positive relationship between the opportunity to save and earn money and participation in collaborative consumption:

- *Hypothesis 1a: Financial Benefits have a positive effect on the Intention to Use Airbnb*
- *Hypothesis 1b: Financial Benefits have a positive effect on the Intention to Use BlaBlaCar*

2) *Service Quality*

The quality of the service of previous experiences impacts users' intentions to continue to use the service (Möhlmann, 2015; Tussyadiah, 2015; Seiders et al., 2007). In fact, when the service quality level is perceived to be high, consumers are willing to continue to use the service. Consequently, the higher the level of the service of previous experience, the higher the individuals intention to continue to cooperate in collaborative consumption:

- *Hypothesis 2a: Service Quality has a positive effect on the Intention to Use Airbnb*
- *Hypothesis 2b: Service Quality has a positive effect on the Intention to Use BlaBlaCar*

3) *Time convenience*

The lack of time people tend to perceive today, makes the opportunity to save time in accessing a product or a service a functional benefit. In fact, as noted by Ganesh et al. (2010) some consumers are willing to pay a higher price just to reduce the time required to access a product. In the same fashion, Hofacker (2001) found that the convenience of shopping without limits on time and space influences the use of online environments. Moreover, Childers et al. (2001) state that "perception of convenience [...] facilitates the accomplishment of the task" (p. 517). Consequently, the convenience perceived in a collaborative consumption platform can influence the intention to continue to use it. As a consequence we posit that:

- *Hypothesis 3a: Time Convenience has a positive effect on the Intention to Use Airbnb*
- *Hypothesis 3b: Time Convenience has a positive effect on the Intention to Use BlaBlaCar*

4) *Enjoyment and positive emotions*

Positive emotions play a key role in determining the decision-making process (Perugini and Bagozzi, 2001). In fact, as found by Huang, Lin and Chuang (2007) the enjoyment perceived in performing a particular activity is a clear example of the intrinsic motivation that drives consumer behaviour. Moreover, some authors (e.g. Babin, Darden and Griffin, 1994) find that in shopping activities, even though the buying process can be perceived as work, the consumer might enjoy it, while Van der Heiden (2004) found enjoyment as one of the main factors that influences the use of the information system. In collaborative consumption literature, John (2013) states that collaborative consumption "is about enjoying shared access to a commonly-owned good". Recently, Hamari, Sjöklint and Ukkonen (2016) have found that enjoyment is the main predictor of the intention to participate in collaborative consumption. In a similar way, we hypothesise that even if collaborative consumption includes a component of work, it can still be perceived as enjoyable, and consequently positively influences the intention to take part in peer-to-peer sharing. We thus postulate that:

- *Hypothesis 4a: Enjoyment has a positive effect on the Intention to Use Airbnb*
- *Hypothesis 4b: Enjoyment has a positive effect on the Intention to Use BlaBlaCar*

5) Social Benefits

The digital literature is starting to show the ability of the Internet to allow social interaction. Consumers communicate online to share opinions and rewards that produce both economic benefits (Money) and social benefits (Gift) (Pellegrini and De Canio, 2016). Besides facilitating the spread of new business models, the Internet is creating new forms of social interaction. Thanks to the sharing nature of collaborative consumption, benefits deriving from social interaction influence resource circulation and user interest in accessing the service (Arnould and Rose, 2016; Tussyadiah, 2015; Belk, 2010). As stated by Heo (2016), individuals participate in collaborative consumption in order to exchange value derived from interaction, feeling themselves to be active partners in value creation.

- *Hypothesis 5a: Social Benefits have a positive effect on the Intention to Use Airbnb*
- *Hypothesis 5b: Social Benefits have a positive effect on the Intention to Use BlaBlaCar*

6) Social Responsibility

According to the work of Botsam and Rogers (2010) collaborative consumption implies trust in strangers. Indeed, as stated by Tussyadiad (2015) using "a peer-to-peer accommodation is to believe that it is safe to spend time in the guest room of a perfect stranger" (p. 5). To reduce inherent risk, collaborative consumption platforms, like other digital platforms, have introduced a peer-to-peer review system that allows users to evaluate their previous experiences. In this way platforms make it possible to increase the social responsibility of hosts and guests, and drivers and passengers. A survey carried out by BlaBlaCar found their drivers to be better behaved than other drivers, as a result of their responsibility towards passengers. We can thus postulate that social responsibility, by increasing service quality, has a positive effect on the intention to continue to use the service, as follows:

- *Hypothesis 6a: Social Responsibility has a positive effect on the Intention to Use Airbnb*
- *Hypothesis 6b: Social Responsibility has a positive effect on the Intention to Use BlaBlaCar*

7) Environmental Sustainability

One of the most frequent reasons given for individual participation in collaborative consumption is the preservation of the environment (*e.g.* John, 2013; Lamberton and Rose, 2012; Belk, 2010). In the shift towards a more sustainable society, people are finding more efficient ways to use resources in order to reduce waste (Gansky, 2010). Collaborative consumption participation is generally linked with the ideology of environmentally aware consumption (Hamari, Sjöklint and Ukkonen, 2016), and in modern society there is a new approach to redistribution aiming to enhance sustainability by deploying access to resources (Tussyadiah, 2015). As a consequence, a higher level of sustainable consumption awareness may increase users' intention to use collaborative consumption platforms. Thus, we posit that:

- *Hypothesis 7a: Environmental Sustainability has a positive effect on the Intention to Use Airbnb*
- *Hypothesis 7b: Environmental Sustainability has a positive effect on the Intention to Use BlaBlaCar*

6.   Airbnb and BlaBlaCar

Airbnb and BlaBlaCar are two of the fastest growing examples of collaborative consumption in Italy. The empirical analysis below focuses on these two cases, which were briefly described in the previous sections.

To assess the difference in usage of the two services, we ran a survey of actual users who had used the service at least once in the previous six months. We selected only those respondents who use the service at least once per year. This double condition identified those respondents who have good knowledge of the services, and made it possible to identify their reasons for using them.

In total, we collected 406 completed questionnaires for Airbnb users, and 402 completed questionnaires for the BlaBlaCar users. The average age of Airbnb respondents is 38, and for BlaBlaCar respondents it is 37 (Table 1). So collaborative consumption is clearly not confined to young people; it is increasingly used by the whole community.

Table 1   Demographic variables of the sample

		18-30	31-40	41-50	51-60	over 61	Total
AIRBNB	Men	13.3%	22.2%	12.6%	6.9%	1.2%	51.1%
	Women	13.5%	13.5%	9.6%	4.3%	1.0%	41.9%
BLABLACAR	Men	17.2%	22.9%	11.7%	7.0%	1.0%	59.7%
	Women	12.2%	14.4%	8.7%	4.0%	1.0%	40.3%

Differentiating between those that offer the services (Hosts and Drivers) and those that use them as clients (Guests and Passengers), we find that in Airbnb hosts are mainly men with an average age of 39. Similarly, the main drivers in BlaBlaCar are also men with an average age of 39 (Table 2). According to Pagliaro (2015) the average age of the BlaBlaCar passenger in Italy is 34 and the average age of the Airbnb guest is 42. Of these guests, 80% are older than 30 and 56% are women.

Table 2   Demographics in terms of providers and users of the service

		Host& Drivers	Guest& Passengers
AIRBNB	Total	46 (11.3%)	360 (88.7%)
	Men	67.4% (39 years)	56.9 (38 years)
	Women	32.5% (35 years)	43.1% (37 years)
BLABLACAR	Total	51 (12.7%)	347 (87.3%)
	Men	64.7% (39 years)	58.8% (37 years)
	Women	35.5£ (39 years)	41.2% (37 years)

Data provided by BlaBlaCar shows that the average age of male drivers is 37 while female drivers are younger at 34. Passengers tend to be much younger; the average age for both men and women is around 30.

In terms of employment, there are no specific job categories that determine the use of the services. However, as expected, those who have stable professional or white-collar employment are the biggest users (Table 3).

Table 3   Job status of the sample

	Students	Unemployed	Housewives	Professional	Employees	Retired
AIRBNB	6.9%	3.9%	4.7%	26.1%	56.4%	2.0%
BLABLACAR	5.5%	4.7%	4.7%	24.9%	59.0%	1.2%

In our sample, the most common occupations for users are white-collar workers (35%), lower management roles (20%) and Army and Police (15%).

Only 26.35% of respondents say they book stays shorter than two nights, while on average people spend 4 nights for each stay. An important group is people who use Airbnb for stays longer than two weeks. Such people account for just 3% of the sample, but make average stays of 19 days, with a maximum of 30 days. This shows that the initial idea of Airbnb, offering an alternative to traditional hotels, is changing into a room renting service for longer periods. The rise in the use of Airbnb as an alternative for longer stays is confirmed by the blog Jumpshot (2015) which highlights that 15% of the hosts list between 2 and 4 properties.

In the same way, according to BlaBlaCar's own figures, travellers use it to travel an average of 32 kilometres[1] each way, compared to 531 kilometres travelled by our sample. This difference is mainly due to the composition of our sample, which consists of users who have used the service at least once in the last six months and who use the service at least once a year.

In a tendency similar to Airbnb, BlaBlaCar is an example of a collaborative consumption service that is becoming more important as an alternative to other forms of public or personal transport.

---

[1] Data provided by BlaBlaCar on the Italian population.

7.   Results

To verify which of the determinants identified above have the greatest impact on the intention to continue to use the service, Structural Equation Models (SEM) were run for both Airbnb and BlaBlaCar. In the same way as a multiple regression, they measured the weight of each variable and determinant.

BlaBlaCar

The main element that drives the choice of BlaBlaCar is the quality of the service itself (Service Quality → 0.277* → Intention to use BlaBlaCar). The quality and comfort experienced in previous travel strongly influences BlaBlaCar users in their re-use of the service.

A second aspect that strongly affects users' intention is enjoyment (Enjoyment → 0.208* → Intention to use BlaBlaCar). The more the travel is perceived as exciting, enjoyable and fun, the more BlaBlaCar users intend to repeat their experience. There is usually no real discussion of customs and traditions with the other passengers, probably because travel times are short (Social Benefits → 0.117** → Intention to use BlaBlaCar). However, the opportunity to share a journey and meet new people makes a BlaBlaCar trip different from traditional forms of travel. Conversely, social responsibility and the referee system has no effect on the intention to use BlaBlaCar (Social Responsibility → not significant → Intention to use BlaBlaCar).

The economic aspect of BlaBlaCar is only the third element influencing the choice (Financial Benefits → 0.175** → Intention to use Bla-BlaCar).

Contrary to our expectations, the possibility of choosing the departure time and saving time on the journey appears to be not significant in the decision to re-use BlaBlaCar (Time Convenience → not significant → Intention to use BlaBlaCar). As described above, environmental sustainability is thought to underpin collaborative consumption, but, as in the case of Airbnb, it does not appear to influence the choice of using BlaBla-Car either (Environmental Sustainability → not significant → Intention to use BlaBlaCar).

Figure 4   Results for BlaBlaCar users

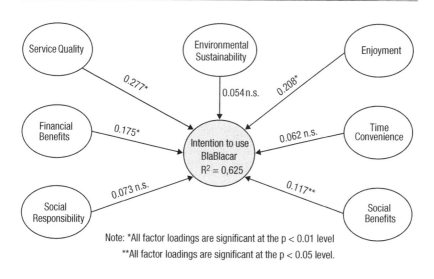

Note: *All factor loadings are significant at the p < 0.01 level
      **All factor loadings are significant at the p < 0.05 level.

Airbnb

Analysing results for Airbnb users, we find a few differences compared to the results for BlaBlaCar.

In the case of Airbnb, we find that the main aspect people take into consideration in evaluating the service as an alternative to traditional hotels and Bed and Breakfasts, is price. The economic value (Financial Benefits → 0.220*→ Intention to use Airbnb) and the quality of the service offered (Service Quality → 0.202*→ Intention to use Airbnb) are the two main elements that influence the intention to continue to use Airbnb. In fact, as noted in the previous chapter, the concept behind the development of Airbnb was, and still is, the opportunity for both hosts and guests to earn or save money.

Positive emotions experienced during the stay have a positive effect on the intention to use Airbnb again (Enjoyment → 0.163*→ Intention to use Airbnb). Another aspect taken into consideration in choosing accommodations are the refereeing system on the Airbnb website. This raises the level of overall social responsibility and has a positive effect on the intention to use the service again (Social Responsibility → 0.143*→ Intention to use Airbnb).

As noted in the Airbnb Report (2016) "the average Airbnb guest spends 38% of their money at local businesses in the neighbourhoods in which they stay". Our results in fact show that the opportunity to mix with the locals and have an authentic local experience is one of the drivers that motivates people to continue to use Airbnb in their travels (Social Benefits → 0.142**→ Intention to use Airbnb).

The ability to reduce time spent booking the accommodation on Airbnb.com is a residual but a positive and significant factor. The user-friendly website and the opportunity to organise travel in less time are two aspects which positively influence the intention to use Airbnb (Time Convenience → 0.097**→ Intention to use Airbnb).

Finally, the use of Airbnb rather than traditional accommodation in 2015 is estimated to have yielded energy savings equivalent to 51.1 million homes and a reduction in waste production of up to 7,300 tons (Airbnb, 2016). We did not however find any significant effect of environmental sustainability on the intention to use Airbnb (Environmental Sustainability → not significant→ Intention to use Airbnb).

Figure 5   Results for Airbnb users

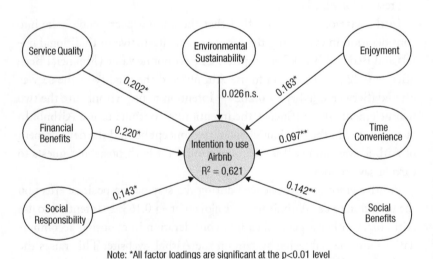

Note: *All factor loadings are significant at the p<0.01 level
**All factor loadings are significant at the p<0.05 level.

8.   Compared findings

In the two studies we can evidence a very good predictive ability of the theoretical models as in both cases the variance expressed by the empirical models is higher than 60% (BlaBlaCar R^2=0.625; Airbnb R^2=0.621).

Moreover, as shown in Table 4, most of our assumptions were confirmed. The only a rejected hypothesis was found in the study conducted on Airbnb users, and unconfirmed hypotheses were found in the study on BlaBlaCar users.

Our analysis shows that individuals involved in collaborative consumption tend to be driven by the opportunity to save money during their travel experiences. In both Airbnb and BlaBlaCar cases, *financial benefits* strongly influence the intention to continue to use the service. However, this aspect is stronger in Airbnb probably due to the higher perception of saving of this particular context of collaborative consumption.

Table 4   Summary of results

Hypotheses	BlaBlaCar	Airbnb
H1: Financial Benefits have a positive effect on the intention to use	Confirmed	Confirmed
H2: Service Quality has a positive effect on the intention to use	Confirmed	Confirmed
H3: Time Convenience has a positive effect on the intention to use	Not confirmed	Confirmed
H4: Enjoyment has a positive effect on the intention to use	Confirmed	Confirmed
H5: Social Benefits have a positive effect on the intention to use	Confirmed	Confirmed
H6: Social Responsibility has a positive effect on the intention to use	Not confirmed	Confirmed
H7: Environmental Sustainability has a positive effect on the intention to use	Not confirmed	Not confirmed

Among economic benefits, *service quality* plays a fundamental role in determining users intention to continue to access to a collaborative service. In fact, service quality that represents the strongest antecedent of the intention to use BlaBlaCar, and has a high effect also in determining the intention to use Airbnb.

Conversely, the *time convenience* shows a weak effect in Airbnb and is found not significant in BlaBlaCar. BlaBlaCar users seem to be less interested in save time during their journey and more influenced by aspects of economicy and quality of the service, as well as the emotions they experiment during the travel.

In fact, the *enjoyment* that is one of the four social benefits investigated shows a strong effect in determining the consumer intention in opting for a collaborative consumption service. In both Airbnb and BlaBlaCar we find a high effect of enjoyment on the intention to use both services.

Also *social benefits* are important in both cases. In fact individuals are looking for an experience that gives different emotions than those given by traditional services; in other words, an experience which enables them to interact and to be active partners in value creation.

A new difference between the two groups is found on the effect of *social responsibility* in determining the usage of Airbnb and BlaBlaCar. Both services have introduced a peer-to-peer review system that allows users to evaluate their previous experiences as to increase the social responsibility of hosts and guests, or drivers and passengers. The relevance of this feature is confirmed in Airbnb but doesn't appear significant in BlaBlaCar.

Regarding *environmental sustainability*, our findings conflict with the theory; in fact we find that the desire for consumption to be sustainable has no influence on choice. In our case studies, platforms inform users that the service is more sustainable than traditional ones, but individuals are not made aware of the environmental impact of their choice.

Given the new trend of environmentally conscious consumption (Tsarenko et al., 2013), it would be advisable for platforms to inform users that the option of sharing their consumption experience can have a big impact on the environment, which can have economic repercussions for society as a whole.

6. Conclusion

This work examines theoretical implications of the new social game. The growing overlap between dialogue and sales, or, more simply, between money and gifts if reshaping the borders between the market and society.

The final goal of the research was to measure to what extent the gift perspective will influence the money perspective. The answers to these questions determine the prevailing model of the new social game in the future.

After the theoretical introduction, chapter 4 leads us into a qualitative analysis of the electronic word-of-mouth (e-WOM) from 20 international crowdsourcing platforms.

The metrics of the co-value model are used to measure and reinforce the basic idea of convergence between the customer perspective – logic of money – and the citizen perspective – logic of gift. The hypothesis of convergence is proven through the analysis of continuous conversation between customers and companies. As shown in the results section convergence is driven by a renewed social sensitivity, which is clearly influenced by collective responsibilities. The new overlap between dialogue and sale generates a positive loop between companies and individuals' responsibility, and reduces the distance between market and society.

It is therefore important to identify the drivers that give individuals a central role in the business model. In fact, individuals' conversations are strongly influenced by the social desire to share personal experiences, knowledge and opinions about the companies or brands with which they interact.

In light of these results in the final chapter we focussed on the Airbnb and BlaBlaCar cases looking for new logical and empirical evidence of the positive convergence between the role of customers and citizens at work.

In these peer-to-peer platforms we assist to the effects of the collaborative consumption.

In fact individuals are called to share not only words but also money since they are both producers and users of products and services thanks to the opportunities offered by new digital platforms. This double role puts into question the borders between the economic and social benefits of the collaborative consumption.

The quantitative analysis confirms that a peer-to-peer architecture is shaped by both money and gift motives. In conclusion, there is no prevalence of money over gift, or gift over money, in motivating the actions of individuals; the two tend to be closely balanced.

In light of both the qualitative – chapter 4 – and the quantitative analysis – chapter 5 – we can suggest that the positive effects of the new convergence will support the growth of new hybrid business models.

The new social game will gradually reduce the distance between customers and citizens. Marketers and researches will be called to understand and influence the change.

References

Aaron R.B., Mathew S.I. (2012). Finding a Home for Products We Love: How Buyer Usage Intent Affects the Pricing of Used Goods. *Journal of Marketing*, 76 (4), 78-91.

Abela A.V. (2001). Adam Smith and the Separation Thesis. *Business and Society Review*, 106 (3), 187-199.

Abela A.V., Murphy P.E. (2008). Marketing with integrity: ethics and the service-dominant logic for marketing. *Journal of the Academy of Marketing Science*, 36 (1), 39-53.

Abruzzese A., Ferraresi M. (2009). *Next. L'identità tra consumo e comunicazione*, Bologna, Lupetti.

Addis M., Podestà S. (2003). Il Postmodernismo: alla Ricerca dell'Introvabile, *Finanza, Marketing e Produzione*, 1 (Marzo). anno XXI, 5-41.

Airbnb (2015) Airbnb's Target Audience. Accessed: 14/11/2016. Available at: https://Airbnb2015review.wordpress.com/2015/07/07/Airbnbs-target-audience/

Airbnb (2016) Overview of the Airbnb community in Italy. Accessed: 22/11/2016. Available at: http://www.airbnbcitizen.com/wp-content/uploads/2016/05/overview_of_the_airbnb_community_in_italy.pdf

Akerlof G., Shiller R. J. (2009). *Animal Spirits: How Human Psychology Drives the Economy, and Why It Matters for Global Capitalism*. Princeton University Press.

Albion M.S. (1983). *Advertising hidden effect*, Boston, Auburn House Publishing Company.

Ancarani F., Costabile M. (2005). Convergenza e strategie di marketing. Definizione del costrutto, esperienze aziendali, domande di ricerca. *Mercati e Competitività*, 2, Milan, Franco Angeli.

Arnould E.J., Price L.L., Malshe A. (2006). Toward a Cultural Resource-Based Theory of the Customer. In: Lusch, R.F., Vargo, S.L. editors. *The Service-Dominant Logic of Marketing: Dialog, Debate and Directions*. (320-333). Armonk, NY, ME Sharpe.

Arnould E.J., Rose A. S. (2016). Mutuality Critique and substitute for Belk's sharing. *Marketing Theory*, *16* (1), 75-99.

Ate Z., Buttgen M. (2009). Customer participation and its effects on service organisations: an institutional and economic perspective. Proceeding Acts, 2009 *Naples Forum on Services*.

Avireddy S., Ramamirtham S.N., Subramanian S.S. Predicting Airbnb user destination using user demographic and session information, San Diego: University of California.

Babin B.J., Darden W.R., Griffin M. (1994). Work and/or fun: measuring hedonic and utilitarian shopping value. *Journal of consumer research*, 644-656.

Bain J.S. (1959). *Industrial Organisation*, New York, Wiley.

Ballantyne D., Varey R.J. (2008). The service-dominant logic and the future of marketing. *Journal of the Academy of Marketing Science*, 36 (1), 11-14.

Bardhi F., Eckhardt G.M. (2012). Access-based consumption: The case of car sharing. *Journal of Consumer Research*, *39* (4), 881-898.

Barthes R. (1987). *Mytologies*. Parma, Pratiche.

Bateson J.E.G. (1983). The Self-Service Customer – Empirical Findings. In *Emerging Perspectives on Services Marketing*, Berry L. L., Shostack G. L., Upah G.D., 50-83. Chicago, American Marketing Association.

Belk R. (2010). Sharing. *Journal of Consumer Research*, *36* (5), 715-734.

Belk R. (2014). You are what you can access: Sharing and collaborative consumption online. *Journal of Business Research*, *67* (8), 1595-1600.

Bendapudi N., Leone R.P. (2003). Psychological Implications of Customer Participation in Co-Production. *Journal of Marketing*, 67 (1), 14-28.

Benkler Y. (2006). *The Wealth of Networks*, Yale University Press.

Bergquist M., Ljungberg J. (2001). The power of gifts: organizing social relationships in open source communities. *Info Systems Journal*, 11 (4), 305–320.

Bettencourt L.A. (1997). Customer Voluntary Performance: Customers as Partners in Service Delivery. *Journal of Retailing*, 73 (3), 383-406.

Bitner M.J., Faranda W. T., Hubbert A. R., Zeithaml, V.A. (1997). Customers Contributions and Roles in Service Delivery. *International Journal of Service Industry Management*, 8 (3), 193-205.

Botsman R., Rogers R. (2011). *What's mine is yours: how collaborative consumption is changing the way we live*. London: Collins.

Bowen D.E. (1986). Managing customers as Human Resources in Service Organisations. *Human Resource Management*, 25 (3), 371-383.

Bowen J.T. (1990) Development of a Taxonomy of Services to Gain Strategic Marketing Insights. *Journal of the Academy of Marketing Science*, 18 (1), 43-49.

Bowen, D.E., Schneider B. (1988). Services Marketing and Management: Implications for Organizational Behavior. In *Research in Organizational Behavior*, B. M. Staw, L. L. Cummings, eds., 10, 43-80.

Bowers M. R., Martin C. L., Luker A. (1990). Trading places: employees as customers, customers as employees. *Journal of Services Marketing*, 4 (2), 55-69.

Braudillard J. (2005). *Violenza del virtuale e realtà integrale*, Milan, Le Monnier.

Brodie R. J., Coviello N. E., Brooks R. W., Little V. (1997). Towards a Paradigm Shift in Marketing? An Examination of Current Marketing Practices. *Journal of Marketing Management*, 13 (5), 383-406.

Burda M.C. (2009). *Cosa fanno le persone quando sono disoccupate*. Proceeding Acts, Festival dell'Economia di Trento, Maggio 2009.

Buttgen, M. (2008). The co-creation of value: emotion, cognition, behavior. Proceeding Acts, Frontiers. In *Service Conference Washington*, October 2008.

Campbell C. (2005). The craft consumer in *Journal of Consumer Culture*, 5, Sage Publications.

Carlson J. R., Zmud R. W. (1999). Channel expansion theory and the experiential nature of media richness perceptions. *Academy of Management Journal*, 42, 153–170.

Carr N. (2008). *Is Google Making Us Stupid?* Article first published online: 9 Dec.

Castells M. (2008). The new public sphere: Global civil society, communication networks, and global governance. *The Annals of the American Academy of Political and Social Science, 616* (1), 78-93.

Chase R. B. (1978). Where Does the Customer Fit in a Service Operation? *Harvard Business Review*, 56 (6), 137-142.

Chia S.C., Chay Y.T., Cheong P.K., Cheong W.Y., Lee S.K. (2012). Fair and Love. *International Journal of Advertising*, 31 (1), 189-211.

Childers T. L., Carr C. L., Peck J., Carson S. (2002). Hedonic and utilitarian motivations for online retail shopping behavior. *Journal of Retailing, 77* (4), 511-535.

Choi N. (2009). *Deriving a new approach for business ethics from the Service Dominant Logic of marketing*. Proceeding Acts, the 2009 Naples Forum on Services.

Costabile M. (2001). *Il capitale relazionale*, Milan, McGraw Hill.

Cova B. (1997). Community and Consumption: Toward a Definition of the Linking Value of Product and Services, *European Journal of Marketing*, 31 (3-4), 297-316.

Cova B., Dalli D. (2007). Community Made: From Consumer Resistance to Tribal Entrepreneurship. In S. Borghini, M.A. McGrath C. Otnes (eds) European Advances in Consumer Research 8, paper presented at the European Conference, Milan.

Cova B., Dalli D. (2009). Working consumers: The next step in Marketing Theory? *Marketing Theory*, 9 (3), 315-339.

Dalli D. (2004). La ricerca sul comportamento del consumatore: lo stato dell'arte in Italia e all'estero in *Mercati e Competitività*, 1, Milan, Franco Angeli.

Daveri F. (2001). Growth and employment consequences of Information and Communication Technologies in Europe, *European Commission, DG Information Society*, (34); Star Research Project, Report 01, May.

Davis F.D., Bagozzi R.P., Warshaw P.R. (1989). User acceptance of computer technology: A comparison of two theoretical models. Management Science, 35, 982–1003.

Dholakia N., Cabusas J.J., Wilcox W. (2009). Consumer, Co-creators. Hackers and Resisters: Conceptualizing Techno-Savvy Resistance to Brands and Marketing. University of Rhode Island, USA. *Advances in Consumer Research Journal*, 8, 241.

Dong B., Evans R. K., Shaoming Z. (2009). The effect of customer participation in co-created service recovery, *Journal of Academy of Marketing Science*, 36 (1), 123-137.

Dujarier M. A. (2009). *Il lavoro del consumatore. Come produciamo ciò che compriamo*, Milan, Egea.

Edvardsson B., Enquist B. (2002). The IKEA saga: how service culture drives service strategy. *The Service Industries Journal*, 22 (4), 153-186.

Elias N. (1988). *Il processo di civilizzazione*, Bologna, Il Mulino.

Fabris G. (2009). *Societing*, Milan, Egea.

Faranda W.T. (1994). *Customer Participation in Service Production: An Empirical Assessment of the Influence of Realistic Service Previews: unpublished doctoral dissertation*. Arizona State University.

Featherstone M. (1991). *Consumer, culture and postmodernism*, London, Sage Publication.

Feldman D.C. (1981). The Multiple Socialization of Organization Members. *Academy of Management Review*, 6 (2), 309-318.

Felix M., Sempels C. (2009). *Service dominant Logic: revisiting the intangibility for a sustainable marketing*. Proceeding Acts, the 2009 Naples Forum on Services.

Firat A. F. (1991). Postmodern culture, marketing and the consumer. In Childers T.L. et al. editors (237-242). *Marketing Theory and Application*. Chicago, IL, American Marketing Association.

Firat A. F., Dholakia N., Venkatesh A. (2005). Marketing in a Postmodern world. *European Journal of Marketing*, 29 (1), 40-56.

Fisher C. D. (1986). Organizational socialisation: an integrative review. In K.M. Rowland G. R. Ferris (Eds.). *Research in Personnel and Human Resources Management*, 4, 101-145.

Fisoun V., Floros G., Siomos K., Geroukalis D., Navridis K. (2012) Internet Addiction as an Important Predictor in Early Detection of Adolescent Drug Use Experience. *Journal of Addiction Medicine*, 6 (1), 77–84.

Formenti C. (2011). *Felici e sfruttati. Capitalismo digitale ed eclissi del lavoro*, Milan, Egea.

Franchi M. (2007). *Il senso del consumo*, Milan, Mondadori.

Freedberg D., Gallese V. (2008). Neuroestetica, Movimento, emozione, empatia. I fenomeni che si producono a livello corporie osservando le opere d'arte, Prometeo Mondadori, 103.

Freeman R. E. (1994). The politics of stakeholder theory: Some future directions. *Business Ethics Quarterly*, 4 (4), 409-421.

Friedman M. (1970). The Social Responsibility of Business is to Increase its Profits, The New York Times Magazine, September 13, 1970.

Frijda N. H. (1999). Emotions and Hedonistic Experience, in *Well-being*, Diener E., Schwarz N., Kahneman D., New York, Russell Sage Foundation.

Fuchs C., Prandelli E., Schreier M. (2010). The Psychological Effects of Empowerment Strategies on Consumers' Product Demand. *Journal of Marketing*, 74 (1), 65-79.

Galimberti U. (1999). *Psiche e techne. L'uomo nell'età della tecnica*, Milano, Feltrinelli.

Gallese V. (2008). Mirror neurons and the social nature of language: The neural exploitation hypothesis. *Social neuroscience*, 3 (3-4). 317-333.

Gansky L. (2010). *The Mesh: Why the Future of Business is Sharing*. New York, NY, Portfolio

Gerken G. (1994). *Addio al marketing*, Torino, Isedi.

Gilde S., Pace S., Pervane S.J., Strong C. (2011). Examining the boundary conditions of customer citizenship behaviour: a focus on consumption ritual. *Journal of Strategic Marketing*, 19 (7), 619-631.

Goudarzi K. (2009). The effective of socializing service customers. Proceeding Acts, the 2009 *Naples Forum on Services*.

Grasselli P., Montesi C. (2009). *L'interpretazione dello spirito del dono*, Milano, Franco Angeli.

Grassmuck V. (2013). The sharing turn: Why we are generally nice and have a good chance to cooperate our way out of the mess we have gotten ourselves into. In *Cultures and Ethics of Sharing, by* Sützl W., Stalder F., Maier R., Hug T. Innsbruck, Innsbruck University Press.

Greenfield S. (2000). *The Private Life of the Brain*, Penguin Press Science.

Grönroos C. (2008). Service logic revisited: who creates value? And who co-creates? *European Business Review*, 20 (4), 298-314.

Gudergan S., Wilden R., Lings I. (2009). How does service – dominant logic affect firm performance? Proceeding Acts, the 2009 Naples Forum on Services.

Gummesson E. (2002). Relationship marketing and a new economy: it's time for de-programming. *Journal of Services Marketing*, 16 (7), 585-589.

Gummesson E. (2008). Extending the service-dominant logic: From customer centricity to balanced centricity, *Journal of the Academy of Marketing Science*, 36 (1), 15-17.

Gummesson E. (2008). *Total Relationship Marketing*, III ed., Oxford, UK, Elsevier /Butterworth-Heinemann.

Gummesson E. (2011). 2B or not 2B: That is the question. *Industrial Marketing Management*, 40, 190-192.

Guttentag D. (2015). Airbnb: disruptive innovation and the rise of an informal tourism accommodation sector. *Current Issues in Tourism*, *18*(12). 1192-1217.

Hamari J., Sjöklint M., Ukkonen A. (2016). The sharing economy: Why people participate in collaborative consumption. *Journal of the Association for Information Science and Technology*, 67, 2047–2059.

Hart O. (1990). *Vertical Integration and Market Foreclosure*, Boston, MIT Press.

Heo C. Y. (2016). Sharing economy and prospects in tourism research. *Annals of Tourism Research*, *58* (C), 166-170.

Hirschman E.C. (1980). Innovativeness, Novelty Seeking and Consumer Change. *Journal of Consumer research*, 7 (2), 283-295.

Hirschman E.C., Holbrook M.B. (1982). Hedonistic Consumption – Emerging Concepts, Methods and preposition. *Journal of Marketing*, 46 (Summer), 92-101.

Hirshman E.C. (1986). The effect of verbal and pictorial advertising stimuli on aesthetic, utilitarian and familiarity perceptions. *Journal of Advertising*, 15 (2), 27.

Hofacker C., Pagani M. (2009). Managing Network Services, Proceeding Acts, the 2009 Naples Forum on Services.

Holbrook M.B., Hirschman E.C. (1992). The Experiential Aspects of Consumption: Consumer Fantasies, Feelings, and Fun. *Journal of Consumer Research*, 9 (2), 132-140.

Holt D. B. (1995). How consumers consume: A typology of consumption practices. *Journal of Consumer Research*, 22 (June), 1-16.

Huang J., Lin Y., Chuang S. (2007). Elucidating user behaviour of mobile learning: A perspective of the extended technology acceptance model. *Electronic Library*, 25(5), 585-598.

Humphreys A., Grayson K. (2008). The Intersecting Roles of Consumer and Producer: A Critical Perspective on Co-production, Co-creation and Prosumption. *Sociology Compass*, 2.

Jeong H.J., Lee M. (2013). Effects of recommendation systems on consumer inferences of website motives and attitudes towards a website. *International Journal of Advertising*, 32 (4), 539-558.

John N.A., (2013). The social logics of sharing. *The Communication Review*, *16* (3), 113-131. Available at: http://www.tandfonline.com/doi/full/10.1080/10 714421.2013.807119

Jumpshot (2015) Airbnb infographic: who uses Airbnb and Why. Accessed: 14/11/2016. Available at: https://www.jumpshot.com/airbnb-info-graphic-who-uses-airbnb-and-why/

Kahneman D. (2005). Mappe di razionalità limitata. Indagine sui giudizi e le scelte intuitive, in Motterlini M., Piattelli Palmarini M. (a cura di). *Critica della ragione economica*, 98-99. Milano, Il Saggiatore.

Keh H.T., Teo C. W. (2001). Retail Customers as Partial Employees in Service Provision: A Conceptual Framework. *International Journal of Retail Distribution Management*, 29 (8), 370-378.

Kelley S.W., Donnelly J., Skinner S. (1990). Customer participation in service production and delivery. *Journal of Retailing*, 66 (3), 315-335.

Kelley S.W., Skinner S.J., Donnelly J.H. (1992). Organizational socialization of service customers. *Journal of Business Research*, 25 (3), 197-214.
Kendrick J.W. (1985). Measurement of Output and Productivity in the Service Sector. In R. P. Inman (ed.) *Managing the Service Economy*. Prospects and Problems, Cambridge, UK, Cambridge University Press, 111-123.
Kinney K.M., Grewal G. (2008). Comparison of consumer reactions to price matching guarantees in Internet and bricks and mortar retail environment. *Journal of the Academy of Marketing Science*, 35 (2), 197.
Kollock P. (1998). Social Dilemmas: The Anatomy of Cooperation. *Annual Review of Sociology*, 24, 183-214.
Kozinets R. V. (2002). The field behind the screen: using Netnography for Marketing Research in online communities. *Journal of Marketing Research*, 39 (Feb), 61-72.
Kozinets R.V. (2010). Netnography: The Marketer's Secret Weapon, White Paper.
Kranton R. E, Akerlof G. (2009). Beyond money and markets: identity and social networks in the economy. Proceeding Acts, Festival dell'Economia di Trento.
La Ferla C., Edwards S.E., Lee W.-N. (2000). Teens Use of Traditional Media and the Internet. *Journal of Advertising Research*, 40 (3), 55-65.
La Stampa (2015) Il boom italiano di Airbnb in vacanza a casa d'altri. Accessed: 14/11/2016. Available at: http://www.lastampa.it/2015/07/07/societa/il-bo-om-italiano-di-Airbnb-in-vacanza-a-casa-daltri-4kc8WMbm082rQvca-o4u2dI/pagina.html
Lamberton C.P., Rose R.L. (2012). When is ours better than mine? A framework for understanding and altering participation in commercial sharing systems. *Journal of Marketing*, 76 (4), 109-125.
Leary-Kelly A.M., Wolf S., Klein H. J. Gardner P.D. (1994). Organizational Socialization: Its Content and Consequences. *Journal of Applied Psychology*, 79 (5), 730-743.
Leavy B. (2004). Partnering with the customer. *Strategy Leadership*, 32 (4), 10-13.
Levy Pierre (2008). *Cyberdemocrazia. Saggio di Filosofia Politica*. Mimesis.
Lewin K. (1951). Field theory in social science: Selected theoretical papers. New York, Harper.
Lugli G. (2005). Il prosumerismo nel marketing dei servizi. *Mercati e competitività*, 2. Milano, Franco Angeli.
Lugli G. (2009). *Neuroshopping*, Apogeo, Bologna.
Lusch R. F., Vargo S. L. (2004). Evolving to a New Dominant Logic for Marketing. *Journal of Marketing*, 68 (January), 1-17.
Lusch R. F., Vargo S. L. (2006). Service-Dominant Logic: What It Is, What It Is Not, What It Might Be, in Lusch R.F., Vargo S.L. (Eds.). *The Service-dominant logic of marketing: Dialog, debate, and directions*, M.E., New York, Sharpe, Armonk.

Lusch R.F., Vargo S. L. (2004). Evolving to a New Dominant Logic for Marketing. *Journal of Marketing*, 68 (1), 1-17.

Maglio P.P., Spohrer J. (2008). Fundamentals of service science. *Journal of the Academy of Marketing Science*, 36 (1), 18-20.

Mahadevan B. (2000). Business models for Internet-based e-commerce: An anatomy. *California management review*, *42* (4), 55-69.

Mandelli A., Accoto C. (2012). *Social mobile maketing*. Milano, Egea.

Manolis C., Meamber L.A., Winsor R.D., Brooks C.M. (2001). Partial employees and consumers: A postmodern, meta-theoretical perspective for services marketing. *Marketing Theory*, 1 (2), 225–243.

Martinelli E. (2009). Service Logic Dominant and Retail convergence. Proceeding Acts of the 2009 Naples Forum on Services.

Mathwick C., Wiertz C., de Ruyter K. (2008). Social capital production in a virtual P3 community. *Journal of Consumer Research*, 34 (6), 832-849.

Matofska B. (2014). What is the Sharing Economy? Accessed:28/08/2016. Available at: http://www.thepeoplewhoshare.com/blog/what-is-the-sharing-economy/

McKinsey (2011). *The impact of Internet Technologies*. Free Report.

Michel S., Brown S.W. Gallan A.S. (2008). Service-Logic Innovations: How to Innovate Customers, not Products. *California Management Review*, 50 (3).

Mills P.K., Morris J.H. (1986). Clients as 'Partial' Employees of Service Organizations: Role Development in Client Participation. *Academy of Management Review*, 11 (4), 726-735.

Möhlmann M. (2015). Collaborative consumption: determinants of satisfaction and the likelihood of using a sharing economy option again. *Journal of Consumer Behaviour*, *14* (3), 193-207.

Montagnini F., Sebastiani R. (2009). Concreate value in retailing: The Eataly Case, Proceeding Acts, the 2009 Naples Forum on Services.

Moriggi S., Nicoletti G. (2009). *Perchè la tecnologia ci rende umani*. Milano, Sironi.

Motterlini M. (2005). *Economia Emotiva*. Milano, Rizzoli.

Nelson P. (1970). Information and Consumer Behavior. *Journal of Political Economy*, 78 (4), 311-329.

Nishiota K., Minami K. (2009). New Roles of Interfirm Relationships in Service Developments: The Case of the Japanese ICT Industry, Proceeding Acts, the 2009 Naples Forum on Services.

Novak T.P., Hoffman D.L., Yung Y.F. (2000). Measuring the Customer Experience in Online Environments: a Structural Modelling Approach. *Marketing Science*, 19 (1 Winter), 22-44.

Nunnally J.C., Bernstein I.H. (1994). *Psychometric Theory*. New York, Mcgraw-Hill.

Olleros F.X. (2008). Learning to trust the crowd: Some lessons from Wikipedia, International MCETECH Conference on e-Technologies.

Pagani M., Hofacker C.F., Goldsmith R.E. (2011). The Influence of Personality on Active and Passive Use of Social Networking Sites Psychology Marketing, 28 (5), 441–456,

Pagliaro B. (2015). Il boom italiano di Airbnb in vacanza a casa d'altri. La stampa.it Accessed: 15/11/2016. Available at: http://www.lastampa.it/2015/07/07/societa/il-boom-italiano-di-airbnb-in-vacanza-a-casa-daltri-4kc8WMbm082rQvcao4u2dI/pagina.html

Paulin M., Ferguson R.J., Bergeron J. (2006). Service climate and organizational commitment: The importance of customer linkages. *Journal of Business Research*, 59 (8), 906-915.

Payne A.F., Storbacka K., Frow P. (2008). Managing the co-creation of value. *Journal of the Academy of Marketing Science*, 36 (1), 83-96.

Pellegrini D. (2001). *Channel equity*, Milano, Egea.

Pellegrini D., De Canio F. (2016). Co-Advertising, E-Wom and Social Responsibility. *International Journal of Economic Behaviour*, 6 (1), 41-58.

Pellegrini D., Minani C., Munehiko I. (2010). Sustainability conscious retailing in green supply chain management: The Case of CRAI 'EcoPoint', Proceeding Acts, Conference Marketing Trends of Venice.

Perrini F. (2007). *Social entrepreneurship. Imprese innovative per il cambiamento sociale*. Milano, Egea.

Perugini M., Bagozzi R.P. (2001). The role of desires and anticipated emotions in goal-directed behaviours: Broadening and deepening the theory of planned behaviour. *British Journal of Social Psychology*, 40 (1), 79-98.

Petre A. (2003). Memorisation non consciente del publicites: apport d'une mesure implicite dans une application au Netvertising, *Revue Francaise du Marketing*.

Pine J., Gilmore J. (1999). *The Experience Economy*, Boston, Harvard Business School Press.

Plé L., Lefebvre I. (2009). *Emergence of value co-destruction in B2B context Emergence of value co-destruction in B2B context Proceeding Acts*, the 2009 Naples Forum on Services.

Plè, L. Càceres R.C. (2010). Not always Co-creation: Introducing Interactional Co-destruction of Value in Service-dominant Logic. *Journal of Service Marketing*, 26 (6), 430-437.

Porter M.E. (1976). *Interbrand Choice, Strategy and bilateral Market Power*, Cambridge, Harvard University Press.

Posner R. (1962). *Antitrust Law: An Economic Perspective*, Chicago, University of Chicago.

Prahalad C.K., Ramaswamy V. (2004). Co-creation experiences: The next practice in value creation, in *Journal of Interative Marketing*, 18 (3 – summer), 5-14.

Prandelli E., Sawhaney M., Verona G. (2009). *Collaborating with customers to innovate*, Edward Elgar.

Pranić L., Roehl W. S. (2012). Development and validation of the customer empowerment scale in hotel service recovery, *Current Issues in Tourism*, 1, 1-19.

Preece J. (2001). Online Communities: Usability, Sociability, Theory and Methods. In, Earnshaw, R., Guedj, R., van Dam, A. Vince T. editors, *Frontiers of Human-centered Computing, Online Communities and Virtual Environments (263-277)*. Amsterdam, Springer Verlag.

Premazzi K., Castaldo S., Grosso M., Hofacker C. (2010). Supporting retailers to exploit settings for internationalization: The different role of trust and compensation. *Journal of Retailing and Consumer Services*, *17 (3)*, 229-240.

Price L.L., Belk R.W. (2016). Consumer Ownership and Sharing: Introduction to the Issue. *Journal of the Association for Consumer Research*, *1* (2), 193-197.

Ravald, A. (2010). The consumer's process of value creation. *Mercati e Competitività*, 1 (1).

Rifkin J. (2000). *L'era dell'accesso. La rivoluzione della New Economy*, Milano, Mondadori.

Rispoli M. (1998). *Sviluppo dell'Impresa e Analisi Strategica*, Bologna, Il Mulino.

Rosemberg N. (1976). *Perspective on Technology*, Cambridge University Press.

Salmon C. (2008). *StoryTelling. La fabbrica delle Storie*, Roma, Fazi Editore.

Sarstedt M., Henseler J., Ringle C, (2011). Multigroup Analysis in Partial Least Squares (PLS) Path Modeling: Alternative Methods and Empirical Results. *Measurement and Research Methods in International Marketing, Advances in International Marketing*, *22*, 195-218.

Schau H.J., Muñiz Jr A.M., Arnould E.J. (2009). How brand community practices create value. *Journal of marketing*, *73* (5), 30-51.

Schmalensee R. (1989). Inter-industry studies of structure and performance. *Handbook of Industrial Organization*, 2 (chapter 16), 951-1009, Elsevier.

Schmitt B.H. (1999). *Experiential Marketing: How to get customers to sense, feel, think, act, and relate to your company and brands*, New York, The Free Press.

Schmitt B.H. (2003). *Customer Experience Management: a Revolutionary Approach To Connecting With Your Customers*. Hoboken, NJ, John Wiley Sons.

Seiders K., Voss G.B., Godfrey A.L., Grewal D. (2007). SERVCON: development and validation of a multidimensional service convenience scale. *Journal of the Academy of Marketing Science*, *35* (1), 144-156

Senadi M. (2009). *Arte e Televisione. Da Andy Warhol al grande Fratello*, Milano, Postmedia Books.

Seraj M. (2012). We create, we connect and we respect. *Journal of Interactive Marketing*, 26 (April), 209-222.

Shepard J.M., Wimbush J.C., Stephens C.U. (1995). The Place of Ethics in Business: Shifting Paradigms? *Business Ethics Quarterly*, 5 (3), 577-601.

Shu S.B., Peck J. (2011). Psychological ownership and affective reaction: Emotional attachment process variables and the endowment effect. *Journal of Consumer Psychology*, *21*(4), 439-452.

Siano A., Vollero A., Palazzo M. (2011). Exploring the role of online consumer empowerment in reputation building: Research questions and hypotheses, *Journal of Brand Management*, 19 (1), 57-71.

Snehota I., Tunisini A. (1999). Relazioni verticali tra imprese e dinamica competitiva, Convegno Aidea, Parma, October, 1999.

Sproul L., Kiesler S. (1986). Reducing social context cues: Electronic mail in organizational communication, *Management Science*, 32, 1492-1512.

Sundbo J. (2009). Innovation in the experience economy. A taxonomy of innovation organisations, Proceeding Acts, the 2009 Naples Forum on Services.

Suwelack T., Hogreve J., Hoyer W. D. (2011). Understanding Money-Back Guarantees: Cognitive, Affective, and Behavioral Outcomes. *Journal of Retailing*, 87 (4), 462–478.

Techcrunch.com (2016). Accessed: 23/11/2016. Available at: https://techcrunch.com/unicorn-leaderboard/

Thurow L. C. (1997). *Il futuro del capitalismo*, Milano, Mondadori.

Toffler A. (1980). *The Third Wave*, New York, Bantam Books.

Tsarenko Y., Ferraro C., Sands S., McLeod C. (2013). Environmentally conscious consumption: The role of retailers and peers as external influences. *Journal of Retailing and Consumer Services*, 20 (3), 302-310.

Tussyadiah I. P. (2016). Factors of satisfaction and intention to use peer-to-peer accommodation. *International Journal of Hospitality Management*, 55, 70-80.

Tussyadiah I.P. (2015). An exploratory study on drivers and deterrents of collaborative consumption in travel. *Information and Communication Technologies in Tourism 2015* (pp. 817-830). Springer International Publishing.

Uber Website – Our story. Accessed: 23/11/2016. Available at: https://www.uber.com/en-IT/our-story/

Uzoamaka A., Jeffrey G. (1999). Effective socialization of employees: Socialization content perspective. *Journal of Managerial Issues*, 11 (3), 315-329.

Valdani E., Ancarani F., Castaldo S. (2001). *Convergenza. Nuove traiettorie per la competizione*, Milano, Egea.

Varian H.R. (2001). *Economics of information technology*. University of California, Berkeley.

Vattimo G. (1985). *La fine della modernità*, Milano, Garzanti.

Vijande, S. M. L., Mieres, G. C. Sanches, L. A. (2009). Innovativeness and firms' valuation of customer and First line employees as co-producer in new service development: impact on performance. Proceeding Acts, the 2009 *Naples Forum on Services*.

Villads Troye S., Supphellen M. (2012). Consumer Participation in Coproduction: 'I Made It Myself. Effects on Consumers' Sensory Perceptions and Evaluations of Outcome and Input Product. *Journal of Marketing*, 76 (2), 33-46.

Virilio P. (1994). *The Vision Machine*, Bloomington, Indiana University Press.

Vital A. (2014). How Airbnb started. Accessed: 22/11/2016. Available at: http://fundersandfounders.com/how-airbnb-started/

Von Friedrichs Y. (2009). Networking as a strategy to business development Collective entrepreneurship, Proceeding Acts, the 2009 Naples Forum on Services.

Weber J.M. (2007). Mirror neuron networks: implications for modeling and consumer behaviour strategies. *Academy of Marketing Studies Journal*, 11 (2), 57-68.

Wikstrom S. (1996). Value creation by Company-Consumer Interaction, *Journal of Marketing Management*, 12, 359-374.

Wikstrom S., Hedbon M., Thuresson L. (2010). *Value creation from a consumer perspective*, Mercati e Competività, Milano, Franco Angeli.

Xie C., Bagozzi R.P., Troye S.V. (2008). Trying to prosume: Toward a theory of consumers as co-creators of value. *Journal of the Academy Marketing Science*, 36 (1), 109-122

Zarantonello L. (2008). L'adattamento della Brand Experience Scale al mercato italiano. *Mercati Competitività*, 3, 109-132.

Zeithaml V.A., Bitner M.J. (2000). *Services Marketing: Integrating Customer Focus Across the Firm*. New York, McGraw-Hill.

Zeki S. (2007). *Arte e Cervello*. Torino, Bollati e Boringhieri.

Appendix (Methodology)

Appendix A – Qualitative Analysis

For Facebook we used Spiderbook, a tool developed by the web metrics company CaffeinaLab. The keyword for the search was the name of the service (e.g. TripAdvisor). Spiderbook yields the public status of users who were then reclassified for the purposes of analysis. The public status shows:

- *No. of friends + No. of friends of commentators (reach)*
- *No. of 'likes' (engagement)*
- *No. of comments (engagement)*: Comments on status have the same audience as the "father status" and no result in terms of engagement.
- *No. of 'share this' (engagement)*

Not all results have the same level of importance. Importance depends on a combination of "reach" (the extent of the audience that could in theory receive the message) and "engagement" (actual reaction on the part of receivers).

Here is an example expressed algebraically. Two statuses – *X and Y* – each describe a variable:

- Status X is written by a boy who has 1000 friends and Y by a girl who has 100;
- X gets 300 likes, 3 comments and 10 shares;
- Y gets 30 likes, 30 comments and 100 shares;

The weight of X is: 1000*300*3*10: *9,000,000* and the weight of Y is 100*30*30*100: 9,000,000. If there are no other comments, the system thus weighs X and Y at 50% each.

For Twitter we used its own search engine selecting "*All*" and set the key word as the name of the service without the hashtag (#). This shows all single mentions. Relevant replies to tweets were also included. The relative weighting of *reach* and *engagement* was carried out using the same principles as for Facebook and the following parameters:

- *No. of followers (reach)*
- *No. of retweets (engagement)*
- *No. of replies to tweet (engagement)*: "Replies" have the same audience as the 'parent tweet' and were given no weight for engagement.
- *No. of "favourites"*, in other word the number of times a tweet was added as a favourite by a follower.

For the search on Google Blog the keyword was again the name of the service. In cases where there were fewer than 200 results, we used any available "Google Suggestions" to insert a term to help the search. If possible we used terms linked to the concept of "opinion", for example "used TripAdvisor", "got TripAdvisor", etc. Comments on posts were also evaluated. For Google Blog, *reach* and *engagement* were measured using a single variable reflecting the number of comments on each message.

In the final weighing, the three sources were given a weight corresponding to the number of mentions in each. The final result, the 'web sentiment', is thus a weighted average of opinions expressed by individual users.

About the Authors

Davide Pellegrini, PhD, is Professor of Marketing in the Department of Economics and Management at the University of Parma where he is coordinator of Executive Programs and Postgraduate Courses in Retail and Distribution Management. His research focused on interbrand competition in a multichannel environment. He was consultant for Iftech, the Japanese Insitutite for Future Technology and awarded the Order des Palmes Academiques in Strasburg. He is founder of *Ti Frutta* the first Italian platform of digital cash back spinned off the University of Parma and controlled by Sia, European leader in technological services for Financial Institutions, Central Banks, Corporates and Public Administration.

Francesca De Canio, PhD, is a Researcher in Marketing in the Department of Economics and Management at the University of Parma. Her research interest lies within the areas of consumer behaviour, digital marketing and multichannel retailing. She spent part of her PhD at the University of Sevilla (Spain) and at the Kingston Business School (UK). She presented in numerous international conferences and published her research and international journals, such as the Journal of Reiling and Consumer Services and she is a member of the Italian Academy of Marketing (SIM) and of the Academy of Marketing (AM).